Timothy Jenkins was trained in anthropol[...] at Cambridge; he served a curacy in Kin[...] was then appointed as Senior Anglican C[...] Nottingham, before moving to be Dean and Fellow of Jesus College, Cambridge in 1992, a position he still holds. He published *Religion in English Everyday Life: an Ethnographic Approach* (Berghahn) in 1999, and was appointed to a university post, as Assistant Director of Research in the Study of Religion, in 2001. He was elected a Canon Theologian at Leicester Cathedral in 2004 (a non-residential, honorary appointment). He is married to Diane Palmer, and has three adult children.

AN EXPERIMENT IN PROVIDENCE

AN EXPERIMENT IN PROVIDENCE

How Faith Engages with the World

Timothy Jenkins

First published in Great Britain in 2006

Society for Promoting Christian Knowledge
36 Causton Street
London SW1P 4ST

'Anglicanism: the only answer to modernity' was originally published in *Anglicanism:
The Answer to Modernity* edited by Duncan Dormor and published by Continuum in
2003. It is reprinted by kind permission of the publishers; 'Ways of living together
– a perspective on Christian marriage' first appeared in *Crucible*, July–September
2005; 'An ethical account of ritual: an anthropological description of the Anglican
Daily Offices' is reprinted by permission of Sage Publications Ltd from *Studies in
Christian Ethics* Vol 15 # 1 pp. 1–10 (© Sage Publications, 2002); this permission is
for non-exclusive world rights in print media in the English language only; 'Church
and intellectuals, nation and state' and 'An Approach to the Millennium or, the first
millennium and the second', were first published by SPCK in *Theology* Nov.–Dec.
1996: 452–6 and in *Theology* May–June 1999: 161–9 respectively, the latter under
the title 'An Approach to the Millennium'.

Scripture quotations are from the Revised Standard Version of the Bible, copyright
© 1946, 1952 and 1971 by the Division of Christian Education of the National
Council of the Churches of Christ in the USA. Used by permission. All rights
reserved.

British Library Cataloguing-in-Publication Data
A catalogue record for this book is available from the British Library

ISBN-13: 978–0–281–05803–7
ISBN-10: 0–281–05803–2

1 3 5 7 9 10 8 6 4 2

Typeset by Graphicraft Ltd., Hong Kong
Printed in Great Britain by Ashford Colour Press

Contents

Introduction

These writings were produced in the course of an apprenticeship, a process they both reflect and reflect upon. That apprenticeship – which is ongoing – concerns my formation as an Anglican priest, and consists at a first approximation in an exploration of the resources to hand in the tradition in order to confront certain problems in the world. In every period, becoming a priest has involved re-learning the tradition and re-imagining the role one has been called to represent; at this time that is certainly a major characteristic of the task. The essential point is that the sort of understanding I wish to convey is inescapably personal and bound up with a narrative: an apprenticeship over time. For this reason, the papers offered here are, with the occasional exception, published in the order in which they were written; the ideas they contain were conceived in response to particular questions and contexts, and were then put to work subsequently in new situations.

An outline of my working life is therefore a necessary preface to these writings, to serve as a frame, and to aid their reading. I was brought up in Oxford, where my father was Fellow and Chaplain of Queen's College, and went to that university as an undergraduate in 1970. After graduating I worked as a social anthropologist, based at the Oxford Institute of Social Anthropology but pursuing first further study and then fieldwork in France. I returned to Britain in 1980, married, and two years later went to Ridley Hall, a theological college in Cambridge; I lived for the duration of these studies with my young family in a near-by village, Comberton. I was ordained in 1985 to serve in the parish of Kingswood in the Diocese of Bristol. I went from there in 1988 to be Senior Anglican Chaplain to the University of Nottingham, and in 1992 was appointed Dean and Fellow of Jesus College, Cambridge, a position I still occupy, though from 2001 I have added the responsibilities of a university post in the Study of Religion.

The papers I include here come from my time in Nottingham and in Cambridge, although they reflect in some cases on experience that goes further back and they draw upon earlier reading. Through these writings there run a number of secular threads – in particular, power, money, sex and time – and a number of Christian themes – for example, reading Scripture, the use of liturgy, the nature of vocation, the place of the local church, and the living of a Christian life. The threads and themes recur and develop through the series, and are found in different patterns. Practically all this material has been created for a specific context, delivered to Church gatherings for various purposes – teaching, training, management exercises, working parties, and sermons. Much of it has been reused subsequently to talk to ordinands about the interest and importance of the work they are to engage in. So not only do the ideas and descriptions emerge to be reused in new contexts, but the papers, too, in certain cases, have undergone recasting. These pieces, then, are explorations of how faith engages with the world, and bear the marks of this process. If there is a constant organizing principle, it is that paying attention to the world is a particular Christian calling, one that I believe to be close to the essence of Anglicanism, and that the descriptions which result from faithful attention may both encourage those in the Church and elicit the interest of those outside it.

I am a hybrid, an academic and a priest. These writings, though they may bear the imprint of an academic mind, come from the priestly part of my work, where a crucial test is the ability to convey meaning clearly. As a consequence, these writings are not scholarly products in the sense of being carefully researched and referenced, but are concerned above all with communication. I have sometimes over-simplified; I have borrowed from all kinds of sources in order to make the point at issue at the time, and what is worse, I have at times lost sight of the original. I have also touched on several areas of which I have insufficient knowledge from a scholarly perspective. These articles – whatever their limitations – are, however, evidence of the kind of questions with which I have been confronted in the course of my ministry, and with which I have had to come to terms. They are responses to demands posed by the situations encountered; the outcomes should be treated as provisional and exploratory, indicative of the kind of thinking needed rather than an attempt to offer authoritative solutions or prescriptions.

It is in this spirit that I offer the following collection. There are many aspects of a priest's ministry that are not touched upon in the pieces, which focus at the interface between the life of the Anglican Church and ordinary life. But these essays are complete and constitute a unity in this sense: every vocation may be called an 'experiment in providence' (a phrase given form in Chapter 2), and this collection is the expression – necessarily fragmentary and open-ended – of such an experiment.

Too many people have been involved in the writing, revision and delivery of these pieces, and over too long a period, for me to be able to acknowledge them all by name. I would like however to record the names of a number of friends, teachers and colleagues who have in particular provided stimulation and insight, support and companionship during my time in Cambridge: Christopher Cocksworth, Jonathan Collis, John Cornwell, Duncan Dormor, David Ford, Dan Hardy, John Hughes, John

Inge, Nicholas Lash, Jeremy Morris, Diane Palmer, Ben Quash, and Janet Soskice. I am grateful for the help of Ruth McCurry and John Welch in the production of this book, and to John Inge for suggesting the project in the first place.

1

Tradition, moderation, kindness and chaplaincy

———◆●◆———

As there is an uneasy spirit abroad of having to offer a justification for oneself, let me address the question, what is a chaplain for? Or, to put it more acutely, why does a university have a chaplain?

If you go round and ask people (as I do), there are three sorts of reason usually offered to explain the presence of a chaplain in the university. The first is *tradition*: put simply, we've always had a chaplain. The second is *moderation*: if we didn't have some mild official person to act as a safety-valve, religion – which can be a dangerous business; you only have to look abroad – might get into the wrong hands and even make itself felt around the place. So chaplains are a species of spiritual bouncer; they are guardians against what Hume calls superstition and enthusiasm: they keep trouble away. And the third reason is *kindness*: chaplains are there for people who like that kind of thing, and for people in distress; to put it brutally, he or she is there for the weak and the weak-minded.

Now all these things are in a sense true, and they are important: although I have put matters somewhat negatively, in fact social morality of any sort is based upon tradition, moderation and kindness, and neither the University of Nottingham, of which I am chaplain, nor any of the halls would exist without a strong dose of all three, as all hall tutors should know.

So they are not bad characteristics to have, and I am very pleased that chaplains are supposed to stand for them and to exemplify them; but I do not think they are sufficient to explain why we have chaplains. On the one hand, everybody must share to some extent in these values; on the other hand, too, chaplains stand for something more, some more obscure values.

I was put on to one way of talking about these more obscure values when I read the recent University of Nottingham *University Plan*, which is a significant theological document.

The *University Plan* quite rightly identifies two fundamental constraints in the life of the university that are to be found not in politicians, finance, ambitions or any such ephemera, but in the nature of things.

5

The first constraint is that matter and history (to put things at their broadest) are full of surprises: so you cannot know what you are going to find out in advance. You have to let your subject-matter lead you where it will. This can be summarized in the slogan 'Truth has its own demands'; or, as the *Plan* has it: the university must be research-led.

The second constraint to which the *Plan* responds is this: although each and every subject has to follow its own nose and see where its subject-matter takes it, nevertheless it appears that there can be cross-fertilization between disciplines, that connections can be made fruitfully, despite the endless fragmentation inherent in being research-led. This is a remarkable thing, for it suggests that at some level things begin to add up, or point to some kind of patterning, even though you cannot say what kind of patterns they might be. There is therefore a real point to interdisciplinarity, and the *University Plan* is also committed (to the best of its ability) to maintaining the full range of disciplines: to keeping the university pointing in all directions.

Now, there are very few explanations as to *why* we have to respond to these two constraints, and historically, the universities' concern with them grew out of the Christian explanation. This is – in short (indeed, in two sentences) – that, on the one hand, because God expressed himself in matter and history, in becoming man, there is no end to the surprises that matter and history can contain. And, on the other hand, because God expressed himself in matter and history, through the Incarnation, all these surprises do not simply multiply away into endless diversity, but also in the end (perhaps with a capital E?) add up to something: they have their beginning and end in Jesus Christ.

You do not, of course, have to subscribe to this kind of explanation in order to do research and to engage in interdisciplinarity – far from it – and, indeed, given the fragmented nature of things as I have described it, one would neither expect nor desire *agreement* on this sort of level. Rather, there are very few ways indeed of expressing these sorts of common values in a university, and Christianity may well be the nearest we have to one. And that is why we have a chaplaincy or chaplains in a university.

Since the world is fragmented, people come to chaplains for all sorts of reasons, most often over what are loosely termed pastoral problems: you will most likely want to speak to a chaplain (in my experience) if you have a tutee who has been bitten by an Evangelical, or who has slept with an incubus, or if you want to get married, or divorced. All that is well and good. You will have an intuitive view of what chaplains are good for. But they are also there, in an obscure and symbolic way, for you to *think with*, if I may put it so – for you to remind yourselves of the central concerns of the university amid the material constraints that the world imposes.

2

An Anglican vocation: chaplaincy as an experiment in providence

———•◦•———

This is a report written at the end of my time at the University of Nottingham; I wished it to reflect upon the principles which had underlain my work as chaplain, and which had emerged more clearly in the course of doing the job. If there is a theme running through all the reports I wrote during my time at Nottingham, I think it is that of exploring the nature of an Anglican vocation.

Paying attention

The first principle may be called paying attention to one's context. The basic premise is that the resources are outside oneself, already there in the situation: it is less one's job to bring God into a place than to discern him in it, and less one's task to gather people together than to discover what they are up to, what moves them and what their desires are. The university in its many parts, or the constellations of people who constitute it, set the agenda and provide the possibilities.

Such a view depends upon two interrelated notions, of embodiment and contingency. For if God is already present in the world, in particular people and situations, one encounters truth rather than constructing it, and matters of great importance impinge upon one, rather than one's discovering them through any act of will or intention.

From this it follows that a major part of the chaplain's task is getting to places you might not expect to find him (or her, but this is largely an autobiographical account). It is no use depending upon friendly or pastoral contacts, and such spontaneous uses that are made of the chaplain; methods have to be developed in order to find out about the university. These methods include visiting departments and administrative offices in a systematic way, and attending formal and informal gatherings of all sorts, such as inaugural lectures, seminars and receptions, as well as pursuing individual contacts. The main point of such an exercise is to become informed, to be in touch with the concerns and pleasures of the place, indeed, to discover its realities and to avoid speculative fantasies. The main theological focus of such an exercise may be said to be a concern with persons: with the patterns of worth, recognition and success – and their opposites – that emerge, with the human potential and limits of each situation, with what can be changed and what cannot.

Two points may be made about such an approach. In the first place, it is a practical necessity. It is necessary because the University has a population of over twelve thousand, very few of whom will seek out a chaplain. It is possible because, almost without exception, people recognize that there is a place for a chaplain; and it is functional because this acknowledged 'right to exist' creates the space that a chaplain can operate in, with both its limits and possibilities.

In the second place, this approach makes certain demands from the point of view of personal discipline. Activity in this case is first of all enquiry, and initiative is going to sites and events organized by other people. Much of a chaplain's work is in waiting for opportunities and in the invisible task of organizing a trajectory, of discovering how, in practice, he gets to places where one would not expect to find him, of researching the questions he wants to ask, the people to encounter and the moments to meet. In this light, activities organized by the chaplain can be a distraction from the real business in hand, a failure of nerve and a retreat from meeting with reality. The discipline is in waiting and paying attention, and 'success' is not masterminding well-attended events, but in finding oneself put to work in hitherto inaccessible places. In short, this approach may be termed 'an experiment in providence'.

Trusting one's fellow-Christians

The second principle is in fact a special application of the first; I call it trusting one's fellow-Christians. By fellow-Christians, I mean the other denominations and in particular their chaplains; the churches, Anglican and others, which, having staff and students in the congregation, have an interest in or concern for the university; and such organizations on campus as the Christian Union and the Navigators. These different groups and the individuals in them will not necessarily share the particular perception of vocation that I have described; they will have different priorities and different contributions to make to the life of the university. Nevertheless, they are part of what is given and a vital resource: both contingent (from a human point of view) and an embodiment of God's presence.

On the grounds outlined above, it is practical to make common cause with one's fellow-believers. Many chaplains seem to have little contact with the bulk of practising Christians in and about the institution; as suggested, the idea is not to ask them to join in with the chaplain's activities, worship and so forth, but to seek where possible to join with them. This policy has practical effects: by getting on terms of trust, it is possible both to offer a more effective ministry within the institution, through co-operation, and to present a common face to the institution, not for purposes of criticism, lobbying or special pleading, but for purposes of witness, presence and mission. I therefore call attention to the importance of this practice, of recognizing our common faith and calling without homogenization (or power games), and of discovering the Christian resources that are already present within an institution.

This business of making common cause with the faith that is there, rather than choosing according to one's own taste, is not optional. The kind of general approach I have outlined could easily lose any specificity or edge, with the chaplain simply becoming a mindlessly cheerful person about the place, or could lead to a defensive and conceited piety of an unrealistic sort (the twin traps identified by Austin Farrer of a liberal emptying out the sense and of Evangelical double thinking).[1] Only by being a part of the body of believers that exists, by being clearly involved and clearly believing something, is it possible to raise the questions that faith poses in the institution. Personally, too, it would be very difficult to sustain the kind of approach I have outlined without the support and help of strong centres of belief, against which to check this style of working. It is worth mentioning that this exploration of trust with my fellow-Christians was an extraordinarily rewarding aspect of my work in Nottingham.

Development over time

The third principle concerns the way that the chaplain's task takes shape through this paying attention to context, and its consequent dynamic or developing nature. It is impossible on these grounds to define in advance what the content or shape should be of the trio of chaplain's aims that I would identify as essential, to wit, conducting worship, pursuing pastoral care, and raising questions of meaning, value and purpose within the institution.

Taking each in turn, worship becomes informed by the experience of the wider context, and develops in style and content with respect to liturgy, preaching, prayer and modes of participation. The life of the congregation also develops in conjunction with this, being concerned with the Christian faith making sense of and in this context.

Pastoral care, from being individual and reactive, becomes to a great extent 'preventative', and on a wide scale. Few people other than the chaplain explore, keep in contact with and monitor the various aspects of university life, though everybody has more specialized knowledge of particular sectors. A major part of the practical value of the chaplain to the institution comes from the unusual range of contacts he has, and the access he enjoys to what is going on, which may be said to give an over-all perspective without *parti pris*. (The only two premises a chaplain brings into play are a concern with persons, and being on the side of the institution, in the Aristotelian sense of seeking its highest good.) There is a pastoral function in taking the different parts of the institution as seriously as do its participants, and keeping an eye upon the consequences, intended and otherwise, of their doing so.

Finally, questions of meaning, value and purpose arise in specific contexts and are conditioned by them. Hence they cannot be posed *in vacuo* or anticipated, only discovered; the questions arise from the concerns of men and women of good will, not from one's own agenda, just as the resources to answer them must come from the people involved.

However, these developments are only a part of the story, for at the same time as the chaplain is pursuing these matters, he is becoming part of the context to which he is paying attention. This is most important. There is a second stage, beyond the initial stage of paying attention, when people of all sorts begin to use the chaplain to think with, in order to articulate or precipitate questions that are present within their institutional lives. At a certain point, people begin to involve the chaplain, to ask him to respond to matters that have emerged in part because of the interest shown in their preoccupations. This process leads to a set of activities of a more or less formal kind, which take time to appear, are not determinable in advance, and demand thought and work. Examples include a seminar with psychologists about what is missing from the discipline from a human point of view, playing the client for a practical class of fifth-year architects, discussing with administrators the provision for student welfare in an expanding university, and talking with planners about the tension between distance learning and the need to create sufficient motivation to study. The theme common to the questions raised around the chaplain is to do with 'obscure values', or questions behind questions: the matters raised are of a second order, as to whether things cohere and make sense, and how to do things better rather than worse within the bounds of the possible. Believers and non-believers raise questions, though in different ways, to the same effect.

At a third stage, it becomes possible to initiate certain matters and to raise questions on one's own behalf or initiative. This possibility is based upon the degree of acquaintance with such matters the chaplain shows and his acceptance, and the matters raised have to make sense within the concerns and values – implicit and explicit – of the institution. I have been struck, however, by the readiness of all sorts of people to take seriously what one has to say, and to create the means to discuss and follow up the topics raised. In this way, it is possible both to respond to certain situations that arise, pastoral and others, and also to share in and contribute to the thinking and activity of the institution; it is also possible to draw upon others to help in one's own thinking in such matters.

As the work progresses, therefore, the three areas of worship, pastoral care and questions become less distinct from each other. Clearly, worship changes as the possibilities and perplexities inherent in the context unfold. But I have also had to consider the pastoral dimensions of learning, teaching and research, to see how the delicate matters of motivation, collective endeavour and participation make their contribution to the university enterprise. One's perceptions are constantly being changed through paying attention to the context, as are one's deployment of energies and time.

It follows from all I have said that a chaplain's task is an example of practical thinking: one's practice is both one's own thinking and part of other people's thinking. Further, it is to do with the recognition of what I call 'obscure values' already present in the institution; it is to do with spotting them oneself (though other people have been doing it better for years) and with helping other people to spot them, so that they may emerge more clearly on the public agenda, at every level. This cannot be achieved for once and for all; it is a continuing task, and I think it involves giving shape or body to two interlocking questions: What is there in a university to have faith in? And what is an appropriate strategy – or 'spirituality' – for contemporary life? Universities, by and large, are not concerned with the Good, the True and the Beautiful, but simply with the Repeatable. People in them experience the call to find something worth believing in; perhaps surprisingly, the chaplain can be an element in this task.

Two further matters

Two further matters are worth raising. First, work with students. Although I have emphasized working with respect to the permanent institution, the principles apply equally to working with students. At the least, one should reflect the institution's values to the extent of taking students as seriously as it does. The main difference to be observed is that students evolve their own perspectives, which may relate only tangentially to institutional questions. Their concerns are to be discovered – once again – by paying attention, not only to academic matters, but also to cultural, political and religious expressions on the campus. These four areas are indeed the traditional materials with which chaplains have worked, but they arise in their specific context, and not in one provided by the chaplains. Involvement in these areas develops as one shows an interest – which, in my experience, is never refused or rejected – and one comes to be used either as a stereotype to think with or as a resource.

The second matter is, what use are chaplains to the wider Church? There are three different focuses, as one moves outwards. First and most narrowly, there is the congregation. The chaplains offer to a group of Christians (normally young adults) training and instruction, an experience of participation and responsibility, and a development of leadership and faith. Some vocations are fostered to the ordained ministry; because of this I was asked to act as a Diocesan Vocations Advisor. Perhaps most vitally, there is the experience that Christianity in its Anglican form makes sense, so that members of the congregation gain a personal faith in a contemporary context, rather than through fleeing that context.

Second, there is the conscious expansion of horizon, so that the Christian faith is concerned with the whole student body and university, and gives confidence to a wide group of Christians, students in particular, beyond the immediate congregation. It does so both by setting an example of what is possible and in dispelling obstacles that tend to confine or divide the public expression of faith. In particular, the business of trusting the faith that is present in the place allows the recognition of a spectrum of possible expressions of faith and the exploration of alliances within that spectrum in such matters as can be agreed upon. These examples of co-operation bear witness to the wider community within the university and avoid any easy dismissal of the claims of faith because of its divisions. More important still, within this diversity of expression, co-operation allows the sharp posing of choice and the demand to make sense to work together, forming a 'common front' that permits the claims of the Christian faith to be made more forcibly than either approach can manage by itself. This appears most clearly when the various denominations' chaplains together support the annual Christian Union Mission. Moreover, this example of co-operation may have consequences for the local churches involved in ministry to members of the university: it may allow rethinking, a recalculation of resources and possibilities, and a relocation of alliances, issuing in an increase in confidence and strength and, quite probably, in long- and short-term recruitment.

Lastly, chaplains pose broad questions about mission and witness to the Church itself. In their work, the matter of the relevance of the Christian faith to a sophisticated part of the modern world is being explored, refined and developed. This is of significance both because a faith that makes sense in a university context leaves the abiding demand that faith should make sense in all parts of life and, more particularly, as the university is a key institution in the reproduction and development of modern society, it suggests ways that the force of the Christian claim to truth can be made felt in that broader society. This work then is helping both to articulate one of the challenges to which the contemporary Church has to respond, and to develop an approach that may help it to do so.

3

Community and vocation

In the previous chapter, I described the Anglican vocation in terms of 'paying attention' to a place and 'trust' in the faith found there. Rather than expand directly upon these ideas, my aim is now to explain the thinking that lay behind this description and, in explaining, to focus upon the connections between a congruent pair of notions, 'community' and 'vocation'.

Knowledge and commitments

To begin with, I have to clear some ground, and to differ from what is widely held to be common sense. In the view from which I differ, the world is taken to be 'out there' and open to inspection. One has to take the trouble to look, examine and test, and then one will know. Knowledge consists in facts, or data, and the person who knows best is the one who knows the most and the latest facts.

This view has wide ramifications. Education, for example, consists in teaching people what is the case, and the best education involves what has been most recently discovered. In this perspective, the world, although extraordinarily detailed, is necessarily 'flat' and uncomplicated, in that it is a single field that will be examined and known in increasing detail. There is no need for any historical knowledge, for as knowledge progresses the past is subsumed into present knowledge, and past knowledge can only be what we might call unreliable data. Further, just as there is very little call to know about the past (except as a private interest), so there is very little concern for the future, which will be like the present, only better. This view suggests a great homogeneity, if I may put it thus: the world is in theory a single space, open to examination or a single gaze, and it exists in a simple time, the linear exploration of that space, or progress.

In this world, commitments are, by their nature, not sufficiently objective to count as part of the given, except as phenomena, so that moral considerations cease to be part of the public, objective sphere and become a matter of individual choice. So one might take up a number of positions – religious, moral, even political – with respect to this single world, but none of them will have any value as 'truth'.

The person who knows has a disinterested gaze, one that is not distracted by passions and partiality. Yet even talk of persons here is a little suspect. For if all there is to be known is data, eventually the 'mystery of personality' will be explained. We shall all be reduced to data, by the progress of various sciences, and our motivations and passions – and, indeed, thoughts and interests – will be revealed to be the result of impersonal processes. So if we know what it is to know, we are a little less clear on who is doing the knowing.

Under these conditions, a characteristic modern spirituality emerges. On the one hand, there is a problem of scale. Impersonal forces control all aspects of public life, and the individual contemplates global problems that appear to be beyond any control. Starvation, ecological destruction, and war, for example, appear to be the result of the summing-up of innumerable disconnected decisions. The world is too large a place for purposive action to be possible, and such action as is possible has hidden consequences. Our only option appears to be to remain as spectators, impotent as to causal powers, blaming anonymous agents supposedly responsible for what is happening.

On the other hand, all that seems possible to us as individuals is a concern with what we might call ethical living. Living in the world of impersonal forces, we make certain personal choices and gestures: we may choose faith, or issue-politics, or various sorts of spirituality, and we submit ourselves to these choices and their demands, in a somewhat unreasoned way, as an attempt to respond to the state of the world as we find it. Personal or arbitrary choice is the only reply we can make to impersonal forces: we do not expect to make a difference, but this is the best we can do.

This spiritual pattern, of a world of impersonal forces and individual ethical living, has similarities with the form of thinking which threatened the early Church, Gnosticism. Gnosticism then and now opposes the material and the spiritual realms, and the aim of the spiritual life is to escape the material, to control the small corner you are in enough to say it has no hold upon you, and to abandon the rest of the world to its fate. As a consequence of this, you lose solidarity with the material world, including the flesh or body, and you also lose any political solidarity with other people, who become part of the problem.

It is not possible, either, simply to turn the whole matter round and to say that the world is good, all will come right in the end, that we are all brothers and sisters, and that this is how God wants things to be – in short, to make a religious identification with progress. Such a move also lacks any grip on reality: as far as we can tell, corruption, apathy, pollution, oppression and so forth are features of this world; to pretend otherwise is to ignore material reality and to leave our fellow men and women to their fate.

Usually we combine the two positions, putting together an unfocused optimism most of the time with a simplifying politics on given issues, usually around a single, transcendent signifier – Class, Ecology, Gender and so on. These are all versions of the same basic spiritual pattern. One might say, in sum, that confronted with the possibility of impersonality being our truth, we rebel, and try and stave off this truth by choosing projects: this part of the world will have value because I choose to give it some; this point of view or analysis is true because I hold it to be so; and so forth.

Such an approach has consequences for faith. In the first place, I choose faith; the decision is mine. Second, faith becomes divorced from experience, and largely a matter of will. It is a way of coping with the world, and not a matter of evidence and reason; faith becomes a matter of what I can bring myself to believe. The believer is therefore insensitive to tradition, unless it is something he or she chooses to believe. Third, the life of the disciple becomes a matter of morality, of changing behaviour; if faith is a matter of what I can bring myself to believe, the life of faith is what I can bring myself to do. Once one concentrates upon the will – or choice – faith becomes a private matter, and beyond any sort of discussion or reason: it is simply what I make myself subscribe to or, in another light, a matter of personal experience, which cannot be communicated, but simply asserted.

At an institutional level, such an attitude licenses a view of religion as an authoritatively revealed set of propositions which cannot be questioned. On what grounds could they be questioned? I will submit my will to whatever authority I choose, either the Church or Scripture, claiming these to be supernaturally outside history and untouched by the progress of knowledge.

There are consequences too respecting the nature of a Christian community and vocations within it. Such a community, first of all, will be defined as a group of like-minded people, people who have made the same choice and commitment. It is therefore an agreeable group, and cannot be a heterogeneous set of people. Moreover, it will be set against the world; such a community will be defined by boundaries, by a common adherence to certain doctrines, styles, authorities and so forth that mark it off from the surrounding society. Herein lies much of the importance of education and training in the faith. Third, this cutting off extends both to the future and the past. The past is unimportant, except for a non-historical deposit of truth-giving authority, and the future is equally so, except as a fantasy of gaining power at the end of history. Lastly, vocation is entirely personal, and the call is to serve the Church community. The world offers neither support nor recognition. Recognition by the Church is a necessary validation only because it is given by like-minded individuals — wherein lie, of course, the seeds of disagreement, for there are no agreed grounds to justify withholding recognition.

Response and discernment

In the *Republic*, Plato contrasts two sorts of empiricism:

> Take our perceptions, then. I can point to some of these which do not provoke thought to reflect upon them, because we are satisfied with the judgement of the senses. But in other cases perception seems to yield no trustworthy result, and reflection is instantly demanded. (VII, 522)

There are some things you look at or inspect; that is the kind of knowledge we have been discussing. And there are some things which cause you to think. This is a different kind of knowledge. I want now to consider this second kind of empiricism, for it is possible that not all the world is passive, laid out, awaiting our disinterested gaze and, indeed, manipulation, but rather that certain aspects of the world compel our response: they evoke discernment and consequent commitment.

The point may be put in this way: although we work with a model of knowledge being demonstrable and certain, in ordinary life we do not deal in certainties of a demonstrable order, but rather in commitments, which we do not choose. We think we make choices, but we never pause to ask what causes us to want. There is a complex process whereby we are summoned out of our sloth and indifference, and become caught up in some practice or other. Until you have been 'summoned', there is no interest in a particular quarter: you may know that other people have a particular interest, but it contains no attraction for you, and you do not bother to find out anything about it. The second sort of empiricism is concerned with something other than disinterested knowledge.

However, once something becomes distinguished from its background for you, and you have discerned that there is something of importance here, consequences follow upon this discernment. For example, what you want, what you know, and what you remember are changed as significance emerges; so future, present and past are altered, as is behaviour. Notice then that this discernment is quite different to the calculation of probabilities, and quite different to habit. Belief is not based upon regularity of occurrence and pattern, but rather upon being seized by a particular truth or insight (or error), however much regularity or probability – and therefore 'experience', in a certain view – stands against it. We are speaking about a certain sort of conviction or commitment.

There are two things to say at this stage. First, whatever it is that causes the discernment, or movement of desire, is outside the person in question. The discernment is the mark within one of something other than oneself. This is important because, although what is at stake is experience, and therefore something private, it is possible to talk to other people similarly affected and to compare notes. There is therefore a possibility of public knowledge based upon this experience of passion, if we pay attention to the conditions of the possibility of knowledge. Second, because the discernment in question has this public or objective aspect, it constitutes groups of people who are subject to it. The discernment then has a power of contagion.

An example may serve to illustrate what I mean. I have begun to think, after years of indifference, that Beethoven's late string quartets are very remarkable pieces of music. As a result, whenever one is played, I go to listen, and there I gather with a small group of people who share the same insight. This example introduces some different notions about vocation and community.

First, I do not need to have a clear notion of what is summoning me. This call is not a matter of will and choice, based upon information, for I am deeply ignorant about the string quartets and could have told you nothing about them to start with except that they compel me.

Second, it is through that compulsion that one becomes involved and begins to investigate and learn; I am called to an apprenticeship, an investigation of the resources and secrets of the sign that summons me. In this investigation, I become altered in whom I associate with, in what I want, in what I know, and in what I remember as significant. Experience itself is structured by living out the commitments inherent in the sign.

Third, membership of the community formed around or by the discernment is not defined by likeness of character, sympathy, or any of the attributes of friendship. It is defined simply by the shared discernment. But the group formed may nevertheless have a structure, and may indeed have the characteristics of what Alasdair MacIntyre calls a 'practice': a group formed to maintain the values which permit the production of the discernment, and its further development and exploration; in other words, a group sensitive to a particular tradition and to the future of that tradition.[1]

Fourth, although the act of discernment is contingent, temporal and partial, the nature of the discernment – or what is discerned – is absolute, timeless and universal. Although music has to be created, produced and reproduced by humans, its value would not be destroyed in principle if nobody responded to it; its 'truth' is not dependent upon human recognition. So it does not matter (in practice) if only a few people share the discernment: although the value is absolute and universal, it does not follow that it must be universally perceived, nor that it shall be. Absolutes of this sort claim only a partial response.

It would be possible to elaborate a view of the world as being organized by such discernments or signs. Such signs may be incompatible one with another, for the apprenticeship of one system may block that of another. In this perspective, the world is not a single open space that can be surveyed by a disinterested gaze, but rather a series of mutually exclusive closed spaces, a series of secrets, though each discernment may be of an absolute or universally valid sort.

Vocations then organize communities around what may be called 'obscure values', signs that lie beyond the obviousness of everyday empiricism. The relationship between vocation and knowledge is reversed: a person does not decide upon an area to investigate and to give value to, but rather is summoned and compelled to learn (given worth – indeed, called into being). Knowledge emerges out of contagion and compulsion, not out of selection and disinterested choice. Knowledge is therefore inescapably temporal in form; one cannot anticipate and map out one's researches in advance, proceeding without error, but can only ever learn too late by reflecting upon experience, recasting one's mistakes in the light of subsequent knowledge. Along these lines, contingency is the mark of truth. Moreover, different knowledges have different times of unfolding.

The communities that are constituted are not, as we have seen, groups of like-minded people, nor defined by boundaries, nor indifferent to the past, nor entirely personal or individual in their understanding of calling. People are bound together by a particular insight, upon which they will still have differing perspectives, although patterns can be discerned and notes compared. The call to minister to that community is the calling to maintain it so that it remains true to its insight. This calling will not then be particularly romantic or communitarian, for these people are not chosen to be together on account of affinity, personality and so forth; nor will it demand singularity in terms of gifts or leadership, for the minister is continually seeking the resources available within the group. The single most important criterion of ministry concerns the promotion of the virtues that maintain the practice and development of the insight in question within its institutional setting.

Marks of the Christian discernment

The letter to the Colossians warns: 'See to it that no one makes a prey of you by philosophy and empty deceit, according to human tradition, according to the elemental spirits of the universe, and not according to Christ' (2.8). If the world is as I suggest, and this is not simply pagan speculation, what are the values of the Christian discernment, and what resources does it bring? In particular, what is distinctive about it, in the face of a multitude of other discernments, and what of its claims to universality?

The Christian faith is that God is to be encountered in the world, and that matter and history have the potential to take part in God's character, will and purposes. In biblical writings, two of the criteria of meeting with God are contingency and pattern; God reveals himself, and this is first of all a surprise from the human point of view, for it cannot be anticipated. And yet, nevertheless, it makes sense in the perspective of God's previous self-revelation, so that things begin to add up, or can be interpreted. God is then to be encountered in epiphanies: glimpses given to us that change us, gather us into new groupings, and set us on to new tasks – the new both recasting the past and being made sense of in the light of it. Indeed, the Gospels (Mark in particular) are organized around the sequence of call, community and commission, the summoning, gathering and sending out of the disciples, with the new emerging on the basis of tradition, which is in turn reinterpreted.

These glimpses, as we know, need not be simply religious in content. The Greeks saw the Divine in terms of the Good, the True and the Beautiful, and any sort of encounter with Goodness, Truth or Beauty will change us, giving us new views, new associations and new desires, so that we see differently, gather with different people, and set about different tasks.

Such glimpses have the characteristics we have described. First, they are glimpses of the real and matter, in the sense that they evoke commitment. There is no choice about such encounters, although there is of course discretion concerning the forms of response. Second, the basis of such glimpses is outside ourselves; they come to us, or are given to us, and alter who we are. Third, they convince us of our solidarity with others. At the least, because they come from outside, we can compare notes with others who share the same discernment, and so investigate what our resources are; moreover, the resources for responding are located in specific, historical communities. So although the matters in question are experienced as contingent, they are not arbitrary in content, and give us some sort of sure ground to go on.

A fourth characteristic of such glimpses is that they are quite small in scale. Part of the Gnostic deception is that the world is 'in general', unfocused and a locus of illusion, and that nothing can be done about it. But the suggestion of glimpses is that people are gathered into relatively small groups by common transforming perspectives, given new aims and purposes in life – or, to put it the other way around, life is to be found in small collective practices or forms of life. This is true whether you listen to music or have faith: something of a specialized or particular nature has got hold of you. Everything worthwhile is experienced in particular, localized ways, although we may also get glimpses through these particular forms of connections, of how what we are on to may be part of something far bigger – even that, in the end, things may add up and that there may be a pattern to everything.

This is the first resource we have: glimpses of any kind, which we check with others, seeking how to express them, finding out what sense they make to and with others, and exploring the terms in which they have been made sense of in the past. Clearly, for a person of faith, prayer is involved, seeking God's will, along with attentiveness to what is given, in worship and the reading of Scripture, and an alertness to the concerns, potentialities and activities of others engaged in faith. Glimpses give us firm ground; they are our experience of the objective and the particular; they save us from caprice, subjectivity or fantasy, as well as from despair and unfocused generalities.

Clearly, however, that is not enough. On the one hand, how do we distinguish what is true, or good, or beautiful, from what is simply fashionable and appealing? How do we escape the fallibility of the human heart? And on the other hand, what is particular to the Christian discernment, or how do we find Christ in the glimpses we are given?

These are not wholly separate issues. Constantly in the Church we meet problems of presentation, of making the faith alive, to ourselves and to others. We need to talk to people where they are, to appeal to them, indeed, to be understood by them, and so to take on contemporary forms. And yet it feels as if, in doing so, we risk the danger of losing what the whole thing is about. There are all sorts of contemporary movements and spiritualities, not simply in eccentric sects but deep within the churches, which raise these sorts of questions of interpretation, gain and loss; to name but three, movements towards health and wholeness, the importation of person-centred psychodynamics, and creation-centred spirituality. How is one to tell whether what these movements have discerned can be seen as Christian? Clearly they possess insights, but are they insights that take us deeper into the matter of our faith? Again, are they based upon genuine discernments (and on what grounds can one discriminate?), or are they passing fashions, with more appeal than goods to deliver, more obviousness than depth?

Here the Gnostic parallel evoked earlier is of help. Many contemporary forms of salvation, whether religious or therapeutic, political or cultural, are deeply selfish, in the following sense. They are focused upon the selfish 'I', its flourishing and escape from contingency. They pursue the flourishing of the self and control over the environment, so that the self is not threatened. Popular movements at the moment promise the Ego that it will escape death, so that at every level of our society there are struggles to establish the freedom of at least a few Egos; economic, cultural, political and spiritual ways of life are formed that conjure away death and limitation for the elect, often at some cost elsewhere.

Christian understanding, however, has been formed against such Gnostic tendencies, for the key to its formulation is faith in Christ and in Christ crucified: the drawing of the selfish self into something beyond itself and its horizons and limits. I put this briefly and in a for-mulaic way because I want to examine certain well-recognized marks of the Christian discernment in terms of the perspective I have been outlining. These marks concern agency, universality and faith – or how God acts in Christ, the scope of his action, and how we take part.

The central point at issue concerning Christ crucified is that, as Paul put it, in the crucifixion Christ became sin for us, or became a curse for us. He became alienated, utterly distant from God. Given that sin may be defined as distance from God, the abandonment of Christ on the cross is critical. In Christ, one might say, sin was fulfilled: one can go no further in the utterly flawed working of things than a man with-out sin being put to death, abandoned by God. In this abandonment he became sin, uniquely beyond God's reach, and in so doing, he fulfilled his Father's will. This is how God has achieved salvation, his form of agency in the world. It means that, no matter how far we go in sin, no matter what is done to us and what we do, to others and to ourselves, no matter how far we go from God, we meet Christ crucified, who became sin for us. There is nowhere, Paul says, beyond the love of God revealed in Christ crucified.

This agency implies a turnabout in our understanding and lives, a dis-cernment or, in New Testament terms, repentance. It is not our task to get to God by striving for righteousness; God has already found us, in our separation from him. This 'being found' we can only glimpse; how could we do otherwise? For the glimpse is that in our separation from God – which is a fact, experienced in our everyday living – we find God, in Christ crucified. This is not a thing to be comprehended by a disinterested glance, but something to take part in, and to explore, and to go deeper into; something indeed that takes hold of you, drawing you into something new: new relationships, new understandings, new desires and new memories, as you are continually recast and set upon new paths. This then is how God works, his agency, which – for all sorts of good technical reasons – is utterly unforeseeable.

It follows from this form of agency that Christ crucified is universal in more than one sense. Christ crucified is absolute in the sense already described: the truth of what has happened exists independently of anybody's discerning it, and it acts, calling forth discernment and consequent commitment from some people, not from all, gathering them into communities with the task of responding, indeed, of worshipping, of expressing and exploring that discernment or depth glimpsed. But more than that, the universality of Christ crucified arises from the fact that all of creation is defined by its distance or alienation from God, the fact that it is not God and does not by nature share in him, and therefore there is nowhere Christ cannot be met with, there is no time or place or event that is not contained or completed in Christ crucified; there is nothing beyond his reach, or that does not finally make sense in him.

Third, the form of our response, or the way that this agency works in us, is through faith. Because Christ is to be found in sin, all life is capable of yielding Christ to us; but because we find him in sin, this finding cannot be by clear sight but by faith. This is why, in the end, one should distrust techniques and methods, forms of knowledge that are supposed to put one on to God, including forms of spirituality. We are concerned rather with contingencies and with discernment, and with taking part through worship and prayer in the life of the collectivity created by the discernment. As that discernment deepens, it expands to include all of life, making alive to us the mystery that God – through Christ crucified – is to be found in everything because everything seems to deny him. Hence the interest in paying attention to the world, and the task of faithful description of aspects of that world, which occupies so many of these essays.

The sort of community formed around such a discernment has at its heart these three marks: the kind of agency at work, the implications of universality, and the life of faith paying attention to the givenness of the world. Each of these criteria of course lacks the obviousness demanded by simple empiricism as a touchstone of reality. The vocation to serve that community then has to cultivate the virtues that promote the life of the community in its exploration of this threefold insight – a community that lives through a power other than its own, that is concerned with the lives of people beyond its boundaries, and that lives by something other than knowledge – while at the same time working with the institutional limitations within which this insight is expressed. It is hard to imagine a more paradoxical task.

Conclusion

According to the view I have proposed, vocation and community come first in the construction of the world and the constitution of an understanding of it, and not afterwards. The common view, which regards vocation as personal and association as voluntary, takes effects for causes and last things as first.

Confronted with the anguish of an impersonal world where the only response seems to be individual ethical gestures, made without hope, I would suggest on the contrary that we see the world not as flat and homogeneous, but as heterogeneous, made up of small practices summoned by compulsions which call forth discernment and commitment. We need to adjust our perception of scale concerning the modes in which significant action is taken, and to deal with particular communities, histories and traditions.

Moreover, I have called attention to the specific form of agency by which God has revealed himself, which defines and creates the Christian faith, the work of Christ crucified. Because of this mode of working, contingencies and compulsions of all kinds are capable of yielding encounters with God. Any particular community of faith then has to pay attention to its context or setting, and to set aside its certainties concerning the adequacy or completeness of its perceptions.

It is for these reasons that I have described the Anglican vocation in terms of territoriality and faithful conversation. 'Territoriality' calls attention both to the scale of the embodiment of insights, and to the need to receive contingency as a vital resource. By paying attention to a particular territory we escape both lack of focus and arbitrary choice in what we give value to. 'Faithful conversation' plays upon the need to pursue this insight without losing sight either of the specificity of faith or of the fact that – because of the nature of that specificity – no one person or group owns or exhaustively understands God's actions in a place. Together, these terms point to the Incarnation and to the mystery of God, to God's self-revelation and absence mediated by faith.[2]

4

Church and intellectuals,
nation and state

————◆◆◆————

A national church?

Coleridge points out in *On the Constitution of Church and State* that, if there is a national Church, it consists not in Anglicanism as such, but in a wider body of what he terms the clerisy, or the clerks: teachers as well as clergy, artists perhaps as well as intellectuals, and, I suppose one might add, civil servants and even journalists. This is the class whose task is the preservation and development of culture, and whose function is the dissemination of that culture throughout the whole community. There is an inescapable political dimension to the clerisy, for only if they perform their task may every person both enjoy their rights and fulfil their duties as a citizen, and the nation as a whole be both permanent and progressive. We must be cultivated (Coleridge suggests) in order to be citizens: education in the broad sense is the key to the reproduction and perfection of the particular society we have.

In this perspective, the Anglican Church is a part of the clerisy but is not, naturally, the whole of it. How then does it fit in? It is important to grasp that each church (or denomination) contains a particular idea of a 'political settlement'; there is at the heart of each a view of how the parts of the social order fit together, their various purposes and rightful functions, and a view too of the place of the Christian faith in that fitting together and right functioning. It is possible that the various ideas of political settlement differ more profoundly between the churches than do divergences in doctrine. Be that as it may, the Anglican Church is in its identity committed to what I shall call a 'liberal settlement'. This is an understanding which affirms the rightness of there being a plurality of viewpoints, which holds therefore with these viewpoints being embodied in a variety of institutions, and which is committed, consequently, to a view of the supreme value of politics, as the practice of achieving compromise between such institutions representing such a plurality of opinions. I call such a view 'liberal' (with a small 'l') because it demands the virtues of pragmatism and tolerance, and the recognition that differences, if they are to be sustained, are interdependent upon each other.

There are strong theological grounds for such a liberal account. Indeed, it derives from two doctrines. The first is that of the mystery of God, which determines that no human description of God can be held to be definitive, to the exclusion of all others. The necessary openness of faith therefore licenses a multiplicity of understandings and forms of participation that need to be held in conversation with each other, while at the same time endorsing a reluctance to declare certainties in matters that are, ultimately, unknowable. This openness underwrites the necessity of there being a plurality of viewpoints in matters of human importance. On the other hand, the second doctrine, that of the Incarnation, points to the fact that humans do have access to the mystery of God, so that one is not left simply with an irresolvable plurality of competing viewpoints, but has the possibility with others of reasoning and building, in short, of embodying something of that mystery and of improving or perfecting these forms of life.

Such an account then contains a particular view of what cultivation or education in the broad sense is: what sort of virtues and opinions should be cultivated; what sort of institutions we are looking for, when people are instructed in their rights and duties; and what sort of culture we are striving to create and propagate. In this way, the Church is the indispensable ally of a certain idea of culture and way of education; it plays its part in the clerisy through the division of labour (which is what one would expect if the vision of society it promotes is true): its task is to pay attention to the claims of faith that underwrite the liberal settlement.

A loss of self-evidence

At present, however, rather than the Church being valued for its contribution in the wider context, the public tendency is to question whether the Church has a value and purpose. There is a loss of self-evidence: my suggestion is that this lack of vision and confidence is a feature not simply of the clergy and the faithful, but of the wider clerisy, or clerkly class. For if the Anglican Church is of its essence committed to a liberal settlement, the present context is one of a widespread decline in commitment to liberal values among the clerks in general, and therefore of some sort of crisis in culture and the values of education.

Talk of decline, although delightful, needs to be substantiated and given a context. I wish, only half seriously, to put it in the setting of a view of the English character, drawn in part from Macaulay. It was from him that I gained the lasting impression that English history is ruled by two countervailing tendencies, which might be characterized as pragmatism tempered by toleration. There is a shifting equilibrium, which may be viewed more or less positively. At times, the English accept oversimple political solutions, but tend to lack the energy to pursue their doubtful compromises to their logical conclusions. At other times, or viewed in another, purer light, the English are rightly distrustful of abstract ideas, and tend to go for solutions that work, and allow a number of viewpoints to be expressed, even if they do not add up in theory. Rather than talk of decline, therefore, we might suggest that the English character oscillates – between amoral pragmatism tempered only by indolence at one extreme, and principled plurality held together by conscious toleration at the other. Both tendencies are present, but one would probably support the latter expression rather than the former and, contrariwise, when amoral pragmatism has the upper hand, there is a decline in liberal values.

The most notable feature of such a decline is a loss of faith in the idea of politics.[1] There is an attenuation of a belief in the virtue of compromise and the value of opinions and approaches that differ from one's own. There is a loss of trust, which is the glue that holds people together as a social and political unit, and this loss is experienced on the ground in a sense of apprehension on the one hand, and a sense of bereavement on the other.[2] The crucial point, perhaps, is that with a loss of politics there is a loss of polity, with a corresponding tendency to break down into smaller-scale tribalisms. That has institutional consequences, for the business of politics increasingly becomes changed into the business of power, or what you can make stick; there is an institutionalization of that loss of trust, reflected and celebrated in such notions as accountability, responsiveness, value for money and efficiency. This situation is characteristic of higher education; higher education lives under and reproduces in its own workings an increasing illiberalism of the state, which might be defined as the strengthening of central powers and the undermining of intermediate institutions.[3]

Most interesting of all, this increasing illiberalism of the state (which is, to repeat, both very English and not at all new) is matched by an increasingly illiberal set of ideologies or mindsets among the intelligentsia, or the clerisy. There are various contemporary ways of thinking and -isms that effectively support and promote this dissolution of the polity, and certainly make it harder to identify the problem in terms that do not reproduce it. A robust defence of the values of liberalism – of tolerance, broad-mindedness and inclusiveness, for example – or an intellectual defence of complexity and interdependence, and their pragmatic consequences, is consequently rather difficult to articulate. It falls within that part of the ideological compass that nobody wishes to come out of: it lies in a poor part of town, an unfashionable *quartier*. Liberalism is not, for example, multiculturalism, nor relativism, nor postmodernism, nor feminism – although it has something to say about how different people might live together, or how incompatible views might co-exist, or how a diverse, irregularly communicative world might co-operate at certain levels, or how the sexes might reach a certain settlement that included emancipation as one of its horizons. In short, liberalism is muted when it comes to posing the important political questions in the public sphere, for the intellectual climate seems to rule them out of court before they are uttered. And if the idea of the liberal settlement is occluded, the self-evidence of the Anglican settlement will be too.

Prognosis

My thesis is then a simple one. (A) The clerisy, in its broad definition, plays an important role in the political life of the nation, a more important role than the members of that class in general appreciate, who have failed, to a degree, to live up to the height of their calling. (B) There are present, however, both in the individual parts and in the whole, the resources to correct the oscillation of the English character in which we are presently engaged. (C) The Church plays its vital part in the clerisy. It needs to keep its nerve and remain true both to its religious principles and to its governing political idea, and in this way fulfil its vocation to the nation, which is to articulate and embody the practical demand of living in love and charity with one's neighbour, with all that that entails.

In sum (and to oversimplify grossly): Up Church, bite clerisy! Clerisy, bite nation! Nation, bite state! State get over the stile, so we may all get home.

5

Two charisms: the Toronto blessing and the ordination of women

———◆◆◆———

Considerable interest has been shown both in the newspapers and the churches concerning the 'Toronto blessing', a Charismatic phenomenon which entered this country from Canada in the early nineties. Although it has been much discussed, both from within the Christian faith – along familiar lines of either 'a manifestation of the Holy Spirit' or 'a deception and a lure for the unwary' – and from a more descriptive, outsider's stance – along the lines of 'extraordinary happenings in London churches' – nobody seems to have raised the question as to why it arrived precisely when it did and why it achieved such an impact.

The 'blessing' is at first sight well defined, both in its characteristic forms and in its origin. It began early in 1994 in a house church that met in a warehouse near the airport at Toronto. However, even the question of origin is disputed. It has been suggested that the phenomenon started earlier, and elsewhere, and has been taken over and managed by the Vineyard churches, a group inspired by the leadership of John Wimber that has been in the forefront of the Charismatic movement for the last twenty years, and which could be perceived to need a new product to maintain its leading role and market share. This language is not used cynically, nor inappropriately, as will become clear. Be that as it may, the Toronto Airport Church is a Vineyard church, and there are a number of such churches in Britain, to which the blessing has spread, and from them to other churches, not only, as one might expect, to those in the house church, Free Evangelical and Pentecostal traditions, but also to churches in the mainline denominations.

The outpouring of the Spirit takes certain characteristic forms. People who have been already once so blessed pray over individuals for their healing, and they in turn become possessed or filled by the Spirit. The body is strongly affected: people fall to the ground and flail, they shake and twitch, or they may appear drunk. It is worth remarking upon the singularity of appearing to be drunk in such surroundings as an Evangelical congregation, especially for women, and also remembering that there is a good New Testament precedent for such appearances. At

29

the same time, the people affected appear to lose mental control, giving vent to uncontrollable laughter, or to sobs, or to animal noises such as roaring. Those concerned say that in these conditions they find refreshment; some experience the closeness of Jesus; some too have visions or receive prophecies.

These features are characteristic in general of Charismatic encounters, except that they are rather extreme, both in the extent of bodily disinhibition and in the degree of their incoherence or incommunicability. These phenomena go a stage beyond speaking in tongues, and interpretations are not offered. Indeed, it is the violence of the phenomena that has surprised even experienced Charismatics. And in part no doubt because of the strength of the phenomena, they are contagious, passing not only from those who pray to those who are prayed over, but also from church to church; people come to seek the blessing and to bring it back to their own congregation. In this way, the blessing draws people and spreads.

It also draws sociologists, who have flocked to these churches; for them too it is a boon, an observable 'religious' phenomenon. I learnt a great deal about the blessing and its reception from papers given at a conference of the Sociology of Religion Study Group of the British Sociological Association in 1995.[1] One interesting angle to emerge is that the churches expected sociologists to come, and have welcomed them. The modern Charismatic leader uses the techniques and findings of sociology and social psychology. There is no fear of 'disenchantment' on the part of these churches; rather they embrace and work with the genius of the modern world. Indeed, they employ strategies borrowed from the sphere of management and marketing. Part of the success of the Vineyard churches has been due to their method of church growth, and also to their degree of openness to opportunities. Wimber, for example, had acted effectively as a consultant to a variety of churches, including Anglican ones. He saw his task as 'equipping the saints': healing church members gives rise to church growth and revival. Church growth and the work of the Spirit can be rationally planned and promoted. For these reasons, the insights of sociologists are not to be feared, but taken on board and put to work.

This openness on the part of Charismatics – which is not of course total, for they select which elements they wish to make use of – is matched by an ambiguity on the side of the sociologists. Although the two male sociologists I listened to who had studied the Toronto blessing in England had not themselves experienced the gifts of the Spirit, and were somewhat reserved in their attitude under the guise of objectivity, several of the women sociologists present were themselves members of Charismatic congregations. They had moved from a stance of objectivity to participant observation, one might say, and were impatient with a sociology that appeared to have no place for belief because it was unobservable and therefore unmeasurable.

Even if sociologists, matching the shift in Charismatic boundaries, have become more open to the phenomenon of belief, likewise they have not had to accept these churches' accounts solely in their own terms. Sociology continues to offer insights which do not necessarily occur to the participants themselves, often by changing the scale upon which observation and comparison is made. So attention is drawn to the terms used, and to the context from which the terms gain their significance, focusing the scale down, from the experience to finer detail, and up, to the wider setting. In particular, at present, sociologists point to the details of body and gender, and to the context of modernity.

Charismatic religion not only adopts modern methods of management and promotion, but also reflects a consumer society that constructs the human person around notions of individual health, prosperity and self-fulfilment. It expresses a contemporary ideal of human flourishing, offering a multiplicity of experiences in a therapeutic context, and emphasizing bodily pleasure rather than bodily control. This is an acting-out of a contemporary version of salvation, of the fulfilment of desire.

There are, as well, other contemporary factors at work. In particular, some images informed by categories of gender are acted out.[2] People who are filled with the Spirit are on the one hand out of control of themselves, and on the other mastered by God. There is an acting-out of disorderliness and irresponsibility that is at the same time pleasurable; the 'drunken' women perhaps epitomize this. At the same time, the congregation is passive, surrendering to a sovereign God who takes people over roughly; in the jargon, you are 'enjoyed by Jesus'. There is, then, as well as a contemporary openness to the body and its experiences, what it might be fair to call a 'feminization' of the congregation, male and female alike, and a corresponding emphasis upon the masculinity of God. This combination gives a clue as to why such a phenomenon should enjoy prominence now. For Pentecostal churches have existed in this country for most of the twentieth century, and this kind of phenomenon is far older; why, then, has the matter come to the fore only in the late 1990s, to be discussed by the newspapers, and by deans and bishops, and by sociologists of religion?

Perhaps the most significant – and controversial – contemporary event in the history of the churches in England has been the ordination of women to the Anglican priesthood. For while the Anglican Church is not by any means the whole of the Church scene in England, it is of particular importance to the public perception of the Christian faith, and the internal politics of the Church of England over this matter have evoked a wide interest and have had consequences beyond its own institutions.

Until the passing of the Measure concerning the ordination of women to the priesthood, Evangelical opponents (on the grounds of authority) looked as if they had a good chance of prevailing because they united with High Church opponents, who opposed the move on different grounds (those of the nature of the priesthood). The alliance gave both parties a greater prominence than they had enjoyed separately for a considerable period, and raised hopes in each case that their wider concerns and agendas would also be promoted. With the passing of the Measure, the alliance has fallen, and there has been a sense of frustration together with a loss of direction, and not only over the cause in question – the expansion of influence and gain in responsibility has lost momentum, and the leadership on both sides has been marginalized, appearing both negative and ineffective.

It is in this context that the violence of the Toronto blessing makes its impact upon certain English churches, with its incoherence, or being without words, its acting-out of women out of control, and its miming of their submission. It is a moment of crisis that is coped with by a re-assertion of the place of women. This context of interpretation may be confirmed to a degree by reactions from elements of the other wing. For among the hopes raised by the alliance against the ordination of women, though not one shared by the Evangelical partners, was the hope of an opening up to or liberalization concerning same-sex relationships, and a wider public recognition of homosexual interests. This hope, too, was frustrated by the breaking of the tacit alliance upon the passing of the Measure: hence, perhaps, the fit of publicly naming homosexual clergy, in an effort to keep open this part of the agenda. It is explicable in the same set of terms as the coming to prominence in this country of the Charismatic phenomena; it is (in a limited sense) a transformation of the Toronto blessing.

Is there a moral to be drawn from this story? It may be that an alliance built upon negatives or opposition is generally poor politics – and may also be poor theology – and in this case was bound to fail in the longer term. But it is more interesting to observe the unexpected consequences of the passing of the Measure. Among these, one can point first to some evidence that the churches are trying to take on board something of the contributions homosexuals might make to the Christian life. And second, in quite another sphere, there is evidence that some sociologists of religion are coming to take up a different perspective upon belief, and to admit their own faith into the frame of reckoning. With two such wonders as these being hinted at, who can doubt what else the Holy Spirit will achieve through the charism of the ordination of women?

6

Buildings and saints: the Feast of Saint Etheldreda

In my attempt to outline the specifically Anglican response to the situation of modernity, I suggest that 'territoriality' and 'conversation' are important to the project. These characteristics point to the fact that the Anglican ministry takes on a certain located population as a given, and tries to discover the life of God in the interactions of the various categories and certainties that make up the place, however inconsistent, incompatible and mutually uncomprehending they may be. This is why an Anglican ministry may be called an experiment in providence.

Such an approach has certain implications concerning buildings, for if you are taking a territory as given, that territory exists in property and buildings quite as much as the more ephemeral human lives that make it up. Yet, by and large, our modern condition tends to look to the existential lives of individuals as the real, and to ignore the constraints and meanings of space and time, represented by property. Indeed, many people in this light regard the church building as an obstacle to and a distraction from the expression of faith, or at best as a depository of superstition which it is one's task to transform or to wean people from.

This is not how I view things and, in any case, when one enters a parish as a priest, one has the responsibility of a church building, or possibly more than one, and it would be as well to have a positive perspective. Moreover, for much of the population, the Church of England exists far more in its churches and cathedrals than it does in any other aspect of its life, and again, one needs to glimpse what such people are perceiving, rather than condemning them as unenlightened. It is un-Anglican to do so, for the reason I outline below in Chapter 14, that we have to take seriously the hard-won collective understandings of modern humanity. By and large, we inside the Church tend to think of it as being made up of people and projects. My point is simply that a certain amount can be learnt from thinking about the building.

Buildings, however, particularly churches and cathedrals, are very complex objects. For instance, they are usually memorials to a particular Christian life, the life of the saint to whom the building is dedicated.

Moreover, that dedication is the product of a particular context and history, the fruit of specific intentions and endeavours. In the construction of the building, giving expression to these intentions and understanding, there are layers upon layers of reference that need to be understood and reconstructed. And then, the buildings have had their effects: these memorials/products/constructions shape subsequent lives and histories, just as they shape and order the surrounding landscape and the village, town or city in which they are situated.

I want to explore these sets of orderings, and how they might bear witness to and participate in the vocation of proclaiming human flourishing and salvation. I shall use a particular example, because in that way we reach the scale at which human meanings are created. I will consider Ely Cathedral, where I once preached at the celebration of the foundress, Saint Etheldreda, and therefore had to think about these questions in a concrete way.

Buildings as human facts

Let us begin from the perspective of modernity. Imagine a spaceship from Mars. It is filled with Martian social scientists, equipped with all their latest measuring devices. It is both invisible and undetectable, which is a great innovation, for it does not disturb the objects under study. It comes and hovers over the cathedral, during the annual service held to celebrate the festival of Saint Etheldreda. It monitors every conceivable phenomenon: the stones, the wood and the glass, the sounds and the smells, the heartbeats and the patterns of brain waves, and so forth. A question arises: would the Martian social scientists be able to understand what a cathedral is, and why people should be meeting to celebrate this festival?

My guess is that they would fail, utterly, and that the reason for this is that a cathedral is a human, and indeed, a divine fact before it is a physical one. A cathedral is a 'condensation of meanings'; it contains a history of human understandings and makings-sense of the Divine – and the Martians have not yet developed instruments capable of reading symbols and their histories. In this sense, maybe, we are in advance of them, although in recent centuries we have perhaps lost some of our perceptive capacities in this respect, and have become alienated.

If we go back to certain tenth-century texts we still possess – rites used in the dedication of cathedrals – we find there a connection consciously made between the cathedral building and the vision of the heavenly Jerusalem, described in the book of Revelation. Medieval cathedrals, such as Ely, were deliberately built upon hills, to serve as emblems of the City of God. The cathedral organizes the space around for

34

miles, drawing the eye and the heart, disposing buildings especially, but trees and fields too, in an invisible grid.[1] And it serves too, in its physical approach from a distance, as a model of the Christian life as a pilgrimage, a series of transformations of perspective, as one draws near to the towers and gates and dazzling walls. Preserving proportions, this is also true for a parish church or the humblest chapel: it orders the place around itself, and gives significance to movement through that place. It is an active locus of meaning.

We have already left our poor Martians far behind. But these New Testament images themselves draw upon Old Testament writings, particularly prophecies and psalms, which dream of the renewal of David's kingdom. Passages which originally referred to the earthly Temple, or to the city of Jerusalem, or to the Hill of Zion, come to have a future reference, so that in the construction of the cathedral, the architects were building not only in stone, but in layer upon layer of images.

Let me give you an example.[2] One such liturgy of consecration begins with verses from Psalm 24, which refers to the ancient processions to the Temple on Mount Zion: 'Lift up your heads, O gates! And be lifted up, O ancient doors! That the King of Glory may come in' (Psalm 24.7). As the service proceeds, reference is made to Jacob's establishment of a shrine at Bethel: 'How awesome is this place! This is none other than the house of God, and this is the gate of heaven' (Genesis 28.17). The two passages are thus brought into relation. The antiphons then speak of Jerusalem, the holy city, Zion, the place where God dwells with the people. The earlier scripture is constantly reinterpreted, by being placed in a new context, and an idea elaborated of the Divine presence in sacred buildings.

Then there follows a reading from the book of Revelation: 'And I saw the holy city, the new Jerusalem, coming down out of heaven from God, prepared as a bride adorned for her husband; and I heard a loud voice from the throne saying: "Behold, the dwelling of God is with men. He will dwell with them, and they shall be his people, and God himself will be with them"' (Revelation 21.2–3). However, we are not dealing, in however sophisticated a fashion, merely with the literal fulfilment of the first Temple. For after this reading there follows a portion of a sermon by Saint Augustine, 'amplifying the awareness that the temple of God is made not of inert rock, but of human hearts and spirits'.[3]

The physical building becomes a figure of the Temple, the dwelling place of God – but also an emblem of the living Body of Christ in stone. An inscription in the cathedral of Saint-Denis reminds those who marvel at the workmanship that the work 'should brighten the minds, so that they travel through the true lights to the True Light where Christ is the true door'. The building itself tells us that a cathedral is made up of living stones, of persons brought to take part in the living Body of Christ. It is possible to suggest, therefore (following Janet Soskice), that the cathedral is an image of the resurrection, and of the resurrected body of Christ.

Human lives as divine facts

To resume my initial starting point, a cathedral is eminently a human fact – and a divine fact in the human – before it is a physical entity. It is quite impossible to understand how such a building came to exist, or even how one stone came to be placed upon another – and what it is, and why it continues to stand, and whether it will in the future – without such ideas as the Temple, the City of God, and the risen body of Christ. These are the names we give to the compulsions that structure human activities, organizing and distributing such 'materials' as wealth, labour and time, as well as stone, wood and glass.

And just as the building can only make sense in the context of such complex human meanings and reorderings, so too with human lives: they are not natural facts, but social facts, created in time indeed by their proximity and relation to such centres of ordering and meaning as this place, just as a human life may be conceived in terms of an approach towards the cathedral building, over the Fens, to Mount Zion.

Considered in this light, a saint's life is supremely a social fact. We indeed recount the lives of saints precisely in this perspective: both as an approach to the heavenly city, and as a mapping out, an inspiration and a guide for our lives. Hence the focus in the service in the cathedral: Etheldreda, Queen, foundress and first Abbess of Ely. There is a point to rehearsing her life, lived out in dedication to the service of Christ, her qualities of austerity and piety, and the miracles that testified to her saintliness, both during her life and afterwards. A life, indeed, that is portrayed in the architecture of the building, on the capitals of the pillars that support the lantern. And we still have the names of some of those whose vocations were bound up with hers, whose stories in her lifetime were guided and shaped by her calling.[4] But that is not all.

Her importance is not solely personal or exemplary, nor simply confined to those who knew her. Her story is part of the pacification of Britain, and the establishment of order, and the role of the monasteries in spreading the Christian faith. She is one of those figures in whom is focused the interplay of religious and political institutions in the attempt to bring about human flourishing: an element in the creation of a Christian Britain, with the possibility of ordered, civilized and faithful lives for countless people. That is the significance of these Anglo-Saxon saints, whose lives are recounted by Bede: we are beholden to them and, in a real way, part of the same project, with the same stakes at issue.

The subsequent history of the memory of Etheldreda is bound up with this project. Her life, her inspiration, has proved a recurrent resource in the place, first in the flourishing community she left behind her, then through the period of its destruction by Danish invaders, after that in the restoration of a monastery in quieter times, the building and rebuilding of first a church and then a cathedral on the site, and in the subsequent life of the building and the place and the diocese. All that history, which leads up to and includes the worship conducted there to this day, only takes the form it does because of the memory and inspiration of that first life, which is recast and put to work in each successive moment. The life of Saint Etheldreda is not simply the memory of her piety, but the inscription of a Christian identity, the holding of the Christian faith in a particular place.

We may say, then, particularly speaking within the Diocese of Ely, that her faith is mother to our faith, and that the cathedral is made up of countless consequent human lives, energies and responses to the Divine that are shown forth in the beauty and materials of the building. And in bringing to mind her vocation we renew our own, in order to share in the life of the New Jerusalem in this particular place, as it shapes everything around itself, catching every eye and heart, and drawing every human life into the life of the risen Christ.

And what can be said of one building, and saint's life, can be said, I think, of every church, whatever its age, complexity, beauty and dedication. Churches are continually renewed constructions of faith, permitting continuities to be made over time in a place, so that lives are lived better, and people come to something. Indeed, churches are to do with the creation of worth, and that brings us to worship, which is the topic of the next chapter.

7

An ethical account of ritual: an anthropological description of the Anglican Daily Offices

Introduction: an anthropological perspective on ritual

Worship is the basic activity and lifeblood of the Church. Substituting the term 'liturgy' for 'worship' gains something in formality and precision, whilst at the same time threatening to lose the sense of intensity or compulsion that the latter carries. By juxtaposing the terms 'liturgy' and 'ethics', we might seek to reconstitute and analyse the way that worship contains and creates worth and obligation. My intention here is to make an anthropological contribution to this project by taking a single case study, that of the Anglican Daily Offices.

An anthropological perspective may help in three respects. First, I shall assume that liturgy can be regarded as a species of ritual, and so that an anthropological account of ritual may contribute to an understanding of liturgy.

Secondly, such an outside gaze allows the drawing up of broad criteria that may have escaped the participants' usual understanding, while at the same time not contradicting or doing violence to their experience. Just as we think we know a ritual when we see one, this appears to be true for informants as well as ourselves. Even if there is no indigenous term for ritual, there are practices that draw attention to themselves, using a number of devices. These are essentially four. To say something is a ritual implies, for a start, that the behaviour appears ordered or structured, and it is repeated. It has a shape, and it is traditional, in the sense of not being 'one-off'. Moreover, if you move from considering the phenomenon at a distance, and ask what the people behaving thus are up to, it may appear that, on the one hand, ritual is often to do with transition, that is, moving from one state to another. And on the other, it involves some sort of extra dimension. It is difficult to express this last feature succinctly. The extra dimension may involve the supernatural, to use one jargon: having to do with God, or gods, or spirits, or ancestors. Or it may not, but it will involve some degree of distancing from the everyday, a dimension of self-consciousness and 'thinking about': an awareness of acting in a ritual fashion as such, a sense of reflection, and a manipulation of 'the social'. For want of a better term, this last characteristic, which has been the object of a good deal of recent debate, may be referred to as 'the transcendent'. The four broad criteria, therefore, are structure, repetition, transition and the transcendent.

The third contribution an anthropological approach may make to the project is to contribute a cautionary note. Despite the rough criteria we have been able to sketch, anthropologists cannot agree upon a definition of ritual, and it is not clear that the broad category sustained by the criteria is itself well founded, or has universal validity. The preoccupation to which the term 'ritual' responds may be particular to us. A recent writer points out that once social scientists, for analytic purposes, separated out thought from action, they needed a mechanism to bring the two back together.[1] And ritual is taken by many social scientists to be precisely the enactment of meaning. Along the lines of this critique, the term 'ritual' may be simply a category created by the investigating community, stimulated by what they take to be the enactment of meaning. And an ethnographic account of a ritual may be nothing more than a re-embodiment of this supposed enacted meaning, a double artefact.[2]

For people such as us, however, of the same background as the social scientists and with the same preoccupations, understanding liturgy as a self-aware enactment of meaning might be a fruitful path to follow. Moreover, it is possible to understand a wide range of ethnographic examples of rituals in this light, as rehearsing a repertoire of ways of making sense of and in the world, simultaneously acting on the world and transmitting these ways of acting. Ritual may be considered as a way of making sense, both passively and actively, construing and constructing.[3] We may map out these activities in terms of our own categories and distinctions, separating, for example, thought from action, or education and intervention, but we are nevertheless mapping out a widespread, and perhaps universal, human activity. We might describe this ritual activity as a 'mechanism for evaluation', for it creates and distributes worth; it discriminates and ranks. It is in this sense that I would claim to give an ethical account of ritual.

At the heart of these specific activities (however difficult they are to specify), there is generally a dominant metaphor or relationship or behaviour which serves as a key to understanding both the specific world-view it sustains and integrates, and those forms that activity and causality take in that world. Through it, all kinds of social and personal relations, economic practices and domestic tasks, political projects and ecological features are implicated, represented and manipulated. In short, in rituals so considered we are dealing with a condensation of identity or, better, a meditation upon being human in a particular form. While there are reasons to be cautious in employing the word 'ritual', there appears to be a widespread class of activities or mechanisms whereby humans create value in the world.

Christian liturgy considered as ritual

If we consider the familiar in the light of the unfamiliar, the practice of various liturgies may be redescribed, employing both the formal characteristics that have been identified and the notion of their providing a particular account of human being. It is clear that Christian liturgies are variously structured, certainly repeated, frequently concerned with transformation, and involved with the transcendent, both in terms of self-consciousness with respect to performance, and in terms of relating to ancestors, gods (or saints), and God. What is more, they are these things in the context of the reiteration of ways of being human. In this respect, they are concerned with the control of boundaries, statuses and definitions, with transitions and the restoration of order. Further, they are capable of taking up every aspect of social life: familial, domestic, medical, ecological, legal, political and economic. And lastly, they integrate nature, culture and the supernatural – or the animal, the social and the godly (including the dead) – in a thoroughly sophisticated fashion.

Through their formality, therefore, Christian liturgies offer a description of 'the way we are'. This account need not be particularly self-conscious, or alternatively, it may be highly contested, and therefore thoroughly thought about. But in either case, it provides a certain 'rightness of fit' that allows participation to make sense or, in another idiom, it constitutes the grammaticality of a range of cultural behaviour and attitudes. This claim suggests a reason why a wide range of people, including those who go to church seldom or not at all, and even atheists, in fact resort to Christian liturgies (especially the Occasional Offices) under certain conditions, and find them satisfactory vehicles for their purposes. The liturgy provides two things. On the one hand, it is a meditation – both individual and collective – upon forms of well-being and dysfunction in that particular social order, simultaneously an inventory and an audit. And on the other, it is a form of activity (as the practical language of the balance sheet would suggest), a positive orientation and intervention in the ordering of the world.

In this account, liturgy operates at both the conscious and the unconscious level, it is concerned with both thought and action, and the participants both act and are acted upon. It is a way that persons together make sense both in and of the social order. Liturgies, in brief, may be considered to be ways of articulating, creating and repeating our own collective becoming-human.

This approach opens up a number of possible projects. For example, I would like to see an anthropological description of the Eucharist in terms of an account of being fully human, for the central Christian definition of flourishing is realized in the particular local circumstances of the gathered believers in the enactment of this rite. And an analysis of the Book of Common Prayer would be desirable, conceived as a linked series of liturgies embodying an integrated view of human order and flourishing.[4]

Let me make two elucidatory points before moving on to the case study that should bear out the broad claims I make for this anthropological perspective on liturgy. First, the BCP is by no means to be written off simply on the grounds of how long ago it was written, and how much the context has changed. For ritual has a power to be conservative and radical simultaneously. In general terms, rituals allow the reiteration of a certain identity in new historical situations, by taking up new elements and both allowing them to read the past and be read by it. Rituals mediate between the past and the future; they may even be how time past becomes the past – in other words, how the past exists in the future, rather than simply being forgotten.

Second, it may be felt that such rituals are incapacitated by their formality and prescribed form. Yet one should note a certain contrast, in different ethnographies, between rituals where form is important, and others where content is. For certain peoples, there is little emphasis upon expertise, upon ritual experts, upon getting every detail right or even upon a strong sense of the boundary between sacred and profane. Nevertheless, such peoples still have rituals, in the sense of loosely structured, repeated events, to do with transformation and the transcendent. What is crucial, it seems, is a certain purity of heart, or honesty of intention in the actors. In contrast, there are examples from elsewhere where the primary demand is for a formal correctness, with a strict observation of stages, order, completeness, roles and boundaries. Such cases, which emphasize prescriptiveness, may make little demand as to conscience; the important thing is to fulfil the form. We might transcribe the contrast (not altogether seriously) in terms of Low and High Church; they are polar possibilities, but not exclusive options. An emphasis upon form in liturgy need not therefore be opposed to the demands of the contemporary world, nor to the expression of sincerity and feeling.

Both these points may be illustrated from the following case study. I wish to consider the form of the Anglican Daily Offices, in particular, BCP Evening Prayer, in the light of all that has been said. These liturgies are not the central Christian enactment of a conception of the human, but rites that presuppose it. Nevertheless, they have a mantra-like quality of keeping a world in being that is worth serious investigation.

The Evening Office in an anthropological perspective[5]

I should make clear that I write both as an anthropologist and as a practitioner, as someone who, in the context of a college chapel, says the Offices. In that context, the contrast mentioned above between formality and purity of intention can be strongly felt. To start with the obvious, during these services, we read the Bible and we pray. And if you wish to read the Bible daily, and pray, you need a structure, both in the sense of a community to support you, and in the sense of a personal habit. One can usually pursue a project by an act of will for a few days or, at best, a few weeks. But in order for an activity to be carried on for months, or years, for a lifetime, or even beyond a single lifetime, there must be a structure to rely upon. Against that, however, we often take the effective saying of prayers to be prevented by structure, because we look for some sort of feeling, spontaneity and, indeed, an act of will, in proper praying. This might be seen as representing rather a Protestant mindset: if you do not make an effort, what is the point? This view may also be understood, however, to be making the valid point that, unless prayers and worship arise out of a particular human context, and respond to a specific situation, they are not real. In the everyday, then, the anthropological perspective which we are bringing to bear is experienced in the question, how does one find feeling, spontaneity and commitment in the habit of the Daily Offices?

The Offices have three obvious preliminary characteristics: they are highly structured, they are repeated, and they are handed on – that is to say, they go on, while the persons saying them may change. As a child, indeed, these same characteristics had struck me: Morning and Evening Prayer are fixed, repetitious and traditional. They are also curiously leisurely, in that they take time to say. This feature is not highly rated in contemporary fashion. Yet, as the writer of Ecclesiasticus reminds us, 'A scholar's wisdom comes of ample leisure' (Ecclesiasticus 38.24). In this sense, these prayers help one to think – which is precisely what my father told me when, as a child, I asked him whether he found saying the Daily Offices rather constricting.

I shall explore in effect how saying the Offices might be said to help one think. I shall approach the question under the three headings I had spontaneously produced in my youthful critic's mind: fixity, repetition and tradition – all of which at the time I thought to be opposed to thinking, which shows what a romantic I was. In fact, we shall see, they also contain such contrary features as flexibility, innovation or the ability to cope with the new, and transformation. And both sides of this series of oppositions are made possible by reference to the transcendent, conceived as the Word of God and the work of the Spirit.

So, first, both Morning and Evening Prayer are highly structured. This makes them, to a degree at least, different to a person's saying their private prayers. But the structure has a very clear purpose, which is to take the participant through a series of steps or stages, so that he or she is transformed: not quite the same person at the end of the process as they were at the beginning. If we take Evening Prayer – in its full liturgical form – it begins with a sentence from Scripture, followed by an Act of Recollection, to remind the participants of what they are engaged in, and proceeds to Confession. There is no point to confession without recollection. Then, an Absolution is pronounced, so that the participants are moved from a state in which matters depend upon their intentions and good will – the business of turning up, and recollecting themselves – to a state of depending upon God's remission of sins: a complete shift in perspective and, indeed, status, a turnaround.

In this absolved state, the Lord's Prayer is said (for the first time) and then the invocatory phrases 'O Lord, open thou our lips' and 'O God, make speed to save us', followed by the Trinitarian formula, 'Glory be to the Father . . .' That is, the participants use what might be called 'primary speech': it is only God in them that opens their lips in worship, and in worship they are caught up in the life and communion of God, Father, Son and Holy Spirit. Praise only comes from God and flows to God, and it is in this Spirit that the Psalm is sung.

The participants' condition is therefore already extraordinarily different to that in which they began the service. And this condition is developed through the reading of Scripture, the Old Testament and the New Testament lessons, to which in each case they respond with praise, through the Canticles (the Magnificat and the Nunc Dimittis). Together, these readings and responses represent a series of steps, an exploration and growth into life in God, under the impulsion of the Spirit. It is only at this stage, in this elevated state, that it is possible to say the Creed, which is far more a profound prayer concerning the life of God and the believer's form of participation in that life than a set of propositions to be construed independently of the context of worship. And in fact, very little makes sense outside the context of worship – but I will come back to that.

It is only now that the participants can say their prayers. They pass through a series of concise formulations, including the Lord's Prayer again, and the Collects. And it is on this 'plateau' that they listen to the Anthem, and the Sermon, and add their own intercessions. Intercessions, indeed, are pretty thin until distanced like this from human wills and intentions – purified and assayed by the work of God. And the Sermon is meant to be a reflection upon what the participants have heard, and what has happened to them, and how that reflects upon and criticizes and transforms the world in which they live: a meditation upon the life of God as they experience it.

So, in sum, the people who go out are not the same as the people who come in; they are transformed – not in spite of but because of the fixity or structure in which they engage. The repetitiveness is not the repetition of the same – 'the thief of time' – but what one colleague terms 'full repetition', creative of time, the creation of the New.

What are we to say then about the repetitiveness of the process? It is perhaps worth saying two things. The first is to echo C. S. Lewis who, in *Letters to Malcolm*, says something to the effect that what every layperson wants out of worship is regularity and predictability, but that he has never met an Anglican clergyman who subscribes to this point of view. That is, the predictability, the familiarity, actually sets one free, to think and to pray: you are not continually negotiating new shapes and contours. To which I must add that such regular worship must still be lively worship. (A good deal could be said about styles of worship, about lively and deadly worship; it is a crucial topic.)

The other thing is that the Offices are not as repetitive as all that. Most importantly, the Psalms, the readings and the Collect change. The Offices are highly scriptural; indeed, there is scarcely a sentence in them that is not either directly taken from, or else echoes, the Bible, in particular, the Psalms. They are therefore, if I may put it so, a vehicle for a daily confrontation with Scripture, and the participants do not choose which parts they hear. This gives a way of understanding the mechanism of the transformation I have spoken of. When Cranmer recomposed the seven Daily Offices into two – Morning and Evening Prayer – his purpose was to remove daily prayer from being solely the task of the priest or religious, and to set laypeople to pray – effectively, all responsible laypersons. And the way that it works is that, twice daily, ideally, the participants, with all their passions, desires, burdens, tasks, responsibilities, relationships and so forth, are confronted with Scripture: not therefore with reflections of the human will and understanding and point of view, but with God's. The participant is given time to think and, as it were, is read by Scripture, rather than the other way round.

It is worth elaborating this understanding a little more. First, how is everyday life passed through this sieve? In practice, there are a series of moves undertaken during the course of the service. The business of re-collection in preparation involves a certain assembling of those persons, causes and projects for whom one has to pray, by each of the small number of people present. In this way, they represent a community. At the same time, each of the persons, causes and so forth is itself tied to larger groupings: the local church as part of the Church in that place, and outward in the rings of the communion of saints; the institutions as part of wider economic, political and other kinds of systems, and so on. There is therefore a set, loosely ordered in a hierarchical fashion, of human groupings brought together and represented by the congregation. This is the raw material whose desires, histories and relationships are brought into confrontation with the Psalms, Scriptures and other materials during the course of worship. And this confrontation issues in the intercessions, which deal not only in local projects and persons, but also in matters of Church and state, and current affairs, sometimes to the surprise of visitors. So there is a quite complex process of construing everyday life, consisting of recollection, representation, meditation and intercession, all conceived in terms of entering into the mind of God, or being read by the mind of God.

Second, the crucial question therefore concerns the reading of Scripture, actively and passively. For the machine at the heart of this process is the active force of Scripture at work, conceived as the Word of God, comforting, confronting and altering the persons involved. This is the mainspring or principle of the ritual, and understanding it gives an insight into the mechanism at work in the liturgy, and the nature of the discipline required. For the process is not a simple dialectic of inspiration and application, but rather involves a more complex, intensive engagement with Scripture. This is the collective business of learning to read: seeing the parallels between, on the one hand, the logic of Scripture in its various parts and their interrelations, and on the other, the logic of the demands of the specific contemporary situation, construed in faith.

I would add, as a practitioner, that we do not always manage this confrontation with Scripture very well, for it demands a collective movement that links intensity of engagement with texts to extensive analogical application. We are indeed constantly looking for a moment in history that makes the Bible our compass, waiting upon the Spirit. But the potential for such a reading is present in every service, and is transmitted by the ritual form. That is one of the functions of saying the Offices: to transmit the potential of Scripture reading us, as well as experiencing that power in fact.

We have therefore reached our third point, which concerned the handing on of the practice. On the basis of this description, we might say two things in conclusion. First, the point of Morning and Evening Prayer being said daily in a place is not simply that the people not present are prayed for, though that happens, as the Prayer Book says it should. It is also that the place (with all its complex multiple locations and moral topologies), in its workings and deliberations at every level, should be leavened by people who have been read by Scripture. Each part of everyday life needs to be touched in this way, so that it is not simply a matter of the struggle of human desires and understandings and memories, but is shaped by something more, something else.

To develop this point: it is clear that in participating in modern life, and the running of complex institutions, every adult person is simultaneously confronted by responsibilities and demands, and lacks sufficient knowledge to respond to them in a reasonable way. This is a condition of life. It means that responses to situations are normally inadequate, and usually contain unforeseen consequences of a kind that often reproduce the problems they were meant to resolve. This feature of replication is not least because the persons responding have not examined their unconscious presuppositions and desires, nor considered the formation of their motivations. In these circumstances, any management consultant worth their salt would prescribe the need for a small-scale, repetitive technique that allowed groups of persons making decisions or taking responsibility to assay their feelings, themselves and their situation. They would need a daily way of reckoning their confusion or lack of clarity by confronting it with an external mind, or source of order. We ourselves are certainly in need of something resembling the Daily Offices, to be able to steer whatever barque we are responsible for with some hope of arriving at port, rather than foundering or sinking.

Now if that is the function of the daily repetition of the Offices, and how they work, it must immediately be said that relatively few laypeople are engaged in this collective prayer. But these prayers also have a representative function which should not be underestimated, and my concluding point relates to this. The fact is that the repetition of prayer, the leavening and transforming role of worship, has always been a tenuous thread amongst the life of any institution, people or society. But it is nonetheless vital, and plays a social role for a wider group than the participants. For it represents the possibility, and what is more, the truth, that we are not simply the sum of our egos and strivings, but are capable of extraordinarily more, and indeed are ordered quite differently: our life in fact comes from outside of ourselves, and the key to our lives is gift, not equivalence or calculation. The act of worship makes an anthropological claim about what is the case concerning the definition of the human.

This claim refers back to the point that very little actually makes sense outside of a context of worship. And tradition, in the sense of this life, lives in the performers of it. The performers of liturgy are in continuity with their ancestors, being confronted with the same demand, the

46

same possibility, the same partiality of insight, the same glimpses of glory, that are posed by the character of a life that is not their own, but in which they share through worship. It is this life outside their lives that gives rise to those lives and shapes them, that is borne witness to in the orderly, repeated and traditional worship of the Daily Offices; the reiteration of a collective hope of flourishing, a particular vision of human being.

If the anthropological approach contributes anything to the study of liturgy, it may be said to consist in two movements. There is a distancing from experience that is achieved by considering the elements that make up the process in question. And there is an answering intensification of focus through identifying in detail the mechanism at the heart of the process that articulates repetition and difference. Through this twofold gesture, liturgy and ethics may be rejoined in a more profound understanding of worship.

8

An approach to the Millennium or, the first millennium and the second

---

Chronos *and* kairos

How are we to think about the Millennium? This article was originally written in the period leading up to the year 2000, when a certain
spectrum of characteristic problems was emerging concerning how to
understand the event. As a first approach, the Millennium offered what
we may call an 'empty form'. By this, I mean two things. First, that it
had a force of its own; it posed a demand, and could not be ignored.
Many people would have liked to ignore it, to pretend it was not happening, or to claim it was of no importance, but they found they could
not. Yet, second, despite this force, it could take on many contents, from
cheerful effervescence to apocalyptic doom, from frenetic partying to
hints of the End of Time.

This kind of existence is frequently discussed in terms of the distinction
between *chronos* and *kairos*: the Millennium was not simply a point in a
chronological sequence, but an event. It is because it was both − a date
and something more than a date, an insistence − that it is appropriate
to raise the question of a rite of passage, and the role of different kinds
of time in such rites. For humans mark social calendars by festivals, which
cut into the passage of time conceived simply as mechanical repetition,
and the festivals suggest an irreversible process: the birth of something
new, and the renewal of the old. In this respect, social festivals can be
compared with transitions between social states such as baptism, marriage or funerals. In both kinds of case, there is a marking of events organized through a well-ordered sequence, whereby social order and its
remaking is made real: this is done through formality − dressing up, pro-
tocols, rites and so forth − and its opposite − masquerade − mediated
by a moment of reversal, or inversion. Thus a wedding usually begins
with ceremony and ends in drunken disorder; a New Year's Eve festival
is the reverse, beginning with silly hats and false noses, and ending in
sentimental ceremony. The problem for the organizers of the Millennium
celebrations was then at first sight to find appropriate degrees of for-

mality and informality. The anthropologist Edmund Leach believed – in a materialist mood – that in these celebrations human beings are trying to disguise to themselves the irreversibility of decay and death, by assimilating it to birth and renewal: that linking chronological time and event is a superstitious act designed to cheat death.[1]

Leach then gave the priority, or the reality, to chronology, and suggested that events were a form of illusion. But against this, consider the claim that human beings are constituted by meaning, not by materiality, and therefore by events, for events are essentially to do with meaning. An event has this characteristic: it changes things, so that after it life is no longer as it was before; and it consists in new interpretations, which are expressed in new gatherings or constellations of people, in the emergence of new intentions and desires, and the reformulation of memories, and even in a mutation of categories such as those of causality and time. In fact, continuities, chronological sequences, exist through these recastings, rather than the reverse: our relations to the past and the future are reiterated in such (unrepeatable) events.

The first millennium and the second

The question for present purposes is how we are to understand or interpret the millennial event. It may be taken as read that, as a rite of passage, it was likely to have both formal and informal aspects, awkward protocol and excessive jollity; but how is one to get some sort of fix on what was happening at a more profound level, and the demands of the situation? To begin to develop an answer, let us note, as a symptom of the phenomenon, that it was difficult at the time to say anything new about the millennium; one was besieged with *faits divers*, with miscellaneous news items.

Take this piece of information: the notion of reckoning time by measuring from the birth of Jesus results from the general acceptance of a proposal made by a sixth-century monk, Dionysius Exiguus, a Scythian living in Rome, and this system of dating was agreed in this country at the Synod of Whitby in 664. Let me draw attention to four features of this item: first, the enduring importance of a proposal made by an obscure clerk, whose suggestion emerged in the right place – Rome – and at an auspicious time; second, the lateness of the proposal with respect to the event commemorated (some five hundred and fifty years later): the first millennium is in fact very short; third, the approximateness in any case of the identification of the date – though the imputed four years out is quite impressively accurate for the period; and last, there is an invisible process lying between the proposal and its formal, local endorsement, over one hundred years later, whereby it became acknowledged

as appropriate that time should be measured from the birth of Christ.
Until then, time was generally measured from the accession of an earthly
ruler; our system of dating, in the year of Our Lord, which dates in
Britain from AD 664, takes the same system and transforms it, in ways
that will emerge.

It is a remarkable system of dating that reaches a first millennium
(even when considerably foreshortened), and the first millennium was
accompanied by signs and wonders. The Church had passed through
various millenarian movements, and shed various apocalyptic texts, in
its first thousand years,[2] but it had retained in the canon the book of
Revelation, in the twentieth chapter of which the millennium is ex-
plicitly referred to: the Devil is bound for a thousand years, after which
he will be loosed and, gathering with the Persians Gog and Magog
leading a numberless host, will fight the final battle with the camp of
the saints and the Beloved City, before being finally cast down. This
battle is a prelude to the general resurrection of the dead and the Last
Judgement, when those whose names are not found to be written in
the Book of Life are cast out into the lake of fire, and the New Jerusalem
is let down from heaven to be a dwelling place for the saints for ever.
It is not surprising therefore that the approach of the year 1000 was
awaited with a certain anxiety:

> Some believed the world stood poised on the brink of the millennial reign
> of Christ that would usher in the kingdom of the saints. Others thought
> that the great tribulation was about to begin, and that the Anti-Christ
> would establish his rule over the nations. The army of King Otto I was
> alarmed into insurrection by an eclipse of the sun in the year 968. An
> earthquake in the year 1000 gave rise to panic on a huge scale . . . [This
> anxiety was accompanied by] a preoccupation with predictive prophecy
> and date fixing, flights into irrationality and libertinism, sectarian behav-
> iour, and . . . fundamentalism . . .[3]

Subsequently, medievalists have countered with the suggestion that
nobody would have known it was the Millennium, because for most
people it was much as it always had been, some such date as the thirty-
second year in the reign of King Og. But even the accounts we now
give of the first millennium are interesting: symptoms that serve as signs
of our contemporary concerns.

We are of course more sophisticated than people a thousand years
ago (I write ironically). We have controlled warfare better, we build
better public buildings, our understanding both of God and of human
nature is far more profound, we have eliminated superstition, and so
forth. And very few people expected the coming of either Christ or the
Antichrist in the year 2000. Nevertheless, it is interesting to note that a

number of signs and wonders were anticipated at the second millennium, among them aeroplanes falling out of the sky, a crisis in the banking system, chaos on the international stock markets, global economic depression, food stockpiling, mobilization of troops, even the displacement of populations, famine and war.[4] All of this apocalyptic speculation was fuelled by interested parties: politicians, computer experts, bankers and journalists. But it was curiously similar in some respects to the accounts we give of the first millennium. Those fears, however, were superstitious, were they not? And our fears were perfectly rational, fuelled by our knowledge of computers, and the bugs they have that bite 'em . . .

Categories embodied in time

Two issues need to be raised concerning these parallels. First, most obviously, the year 2000 was two thousand years from the birth of Christ: that is how we measure time (and matters of Common Era represent a – depressingly familiar – missing of the point). There was no other reason for the Millennium, so how best do we make sense of it in terms of Christ? Or, to put it the other way round – and negatively – is it valid to go on reckoning time from the birth of Christ – and if so, is there any other era to which we could appeal?

Second, the reason we anticipated these signs and wonders is that our time has material realizations: it is embodied time, and these embodiments have their consequences. It was indeed no different a thousand years ago: the categories and the materialities were different, but just as real, just as rational, as today's. Hence the categories generated events that bore certain resemblances to those now. So the second question the Millennium posed is this: how will the event of Christ go on being embodied in the materiality of our civilization, in our categories and their realizations? This is a question at a very different level to that of using the occasion of the Millennium to remind people of Christ, or to bring them to Christ: it operates at the level that constitutes the possibility of evangelism, before conscious decision and choice.

These issues – of Christ and the materiality of our categories – together give more focus to the question: how could an appropriate shape be given to the new millennium, a sequence created that should inform and interpret it, a vehicle that could share to a degree both in creating and reflecting the event at issue? The Millennium Dome struggled with the problem of whether it was marking anything above an arbitrary point in a sequence: what sort of continuity, and what sort of event? A representative of the Millennium Commission whom I heard speak felt sure enough about three areas of shared social experience to be able to assume they could be relied upon as a basis for her (vastly expensive) project:

some sort of national identity crisis; the Lottery, or benign chance; and the common decency of people. That is a very sophisticated combination of ideas, yet I doubt whether they constitute any lasting rationale. Nevertheless, the Dome, with its echoes – because of the source of its funding – of the Lottery and chance, still stood as a sign of the birth of Christ. Notions of lottery and chance are for us a luxury, a relaxation from acknowledging the underlying order and potentialities of our civilization. Were the reverse true, and our civilization founded upon chance, there could be no anniversaries, no dates, no points of transition.[5] One cannot reverse the script, and suggest a building to commemorate a thousand years of chance – funded perhaps by that eccentric sect, the followers of Christ, who, by virtue of their superstitious rejection of chance, had unfairly and secretly become very wealthy.

To repeat, the Millennium was not a fact of cosmological Nature, but two thousand years from the birth of Christ. It was at a non-obvious level a sign of sacred time: it pointed to its wider context in that it lies between the Incarnation and the Eschaton. Indeed, it is from these events that it gained its own event-like nature, its faint echo of *kairos*, its whiff not of eternity so much as of judgement. As I have suggested, events refer not to natural worlds, but to worlds of meaning – and natural worlds (contrary to one's intuitions) are secondary to and dependent upon worlds of meaning, functions of worlds of meaning. Ordinary time itself then can serve to raise the question of its own ground, and the Millennium more so; it perhaps is the moment when the non-temporal ground of time rises obscurely into our view. Or to put it another way, the Millennium raised the question – obscurely felt, to be sure – of two thousand years of what? It gave us that queasy feeling that our world of meaning, our order of common sense, our horizon, may be less natural, self-evident and assured than we normally assume. Hence, indeed, the variety of responses offered.

Two ideas from the first millennium

The challenge to the Church in this situation is surely to offer an interpretation of who we are and who God is with respect to us. The Church is the only place that can undertake this particular task; certainly, nobody else is seeking to do it. This challenge points back to the question, already invoked, of the materiality of the categories of belief: how is Christ written into the ordering of everyday life, before conscious choice or articulation?

It is therefore instructive to see what happened a thousand years ago, in the context of the first millennium, when two ideas or interpretations came into view that correspond to the sort of questions that need to be asked. Let us note in passing that while both have enjoyed enormous success and influence, they were articulated by clerks, persons of intellect and prayer.

The first was the idea that the social order comprised three 'estates': those who pray, those who fight, and those who labour. Aldabero, Bishop of Laon, around AD 1025 produced this image of the perfect society, ordered in a threefold or Trinitarian structure: 'triple then is the house of God which is to be thought one: on Earth, some pray, others fight, still others work; which three are joined together and may not be torn asunder, so that on the function of each the works of the others rest, each in turn assisting all'.[6] A similar idea may be found in the works of Aldabero's contemporary, Gerard, Bishop of Cambrai. Together, they produced an image of a society that is 'one and triune like the divinity who had created and would ultimately judge it, wherein mutually exchanged services unified the diversity of human actions'.[7]

This idea has endured remarkably: it was, for example, clearly articulated in the discussions of the right of resistance and the duty of obedience in the sixteenth and seventeenth century, which underlie the birth of the modern world; it is recognizable in the triple structure of Church, Nobility and the Third Estate, which fell at the French Revolution; and it persists even nowadays in talk of the spiritual, political and economic spheres, and the unconscious assumption that they each have their part to play in contemporary social order. To a degree, the idea echoes an even older, Indo-European structure of functions:[8] 'the first, in the name of heaven to lay down the rules, the law that institutes order; the second, brutally, violently, to enforce obedience; the third, finally, of fecundity, health, plenty, pleasure'.[9] But the originality of Aldabero is to apply this trifunctional model to the social body, as a framework for an ideal classification of the kinds of men and of their interdependence, under and in the image of God. In brief, an all-encompassing form of social order – the feudal form, indeed – was imagined and articulated, and found its right time.

The second idea to which I wish to draw attention is equally datable, and also enjoyed a lasting success. It was to a degree dependent upon the first, feudal theory, or an aspect of it (not upon the three orders as such, but upon the principles articulated, of separation, hierarchy and interdependence). It was Anselm's satisfaction theory of the Atonement, centred around the restitution of God's honour, besmirched by man, which appeared in 1097, in *Cur Deus Homo*, probably best translated as 'Why God Became Man'. The argument goes as follows. No human person passes through this life without sin, which is interpreted first as the refusal of a creature to subject his will to God's, and then in these terms: the refusal to give God due honour. For man's sins to be forgiven – and for him to achieve bliss – satisfaction must be made; due honour must be restored to God, making up for the insult by going beyond the degree refused. A violation of God's honour, however, is a violation of supreme justice, and proportionate satisfaction of such a violation is quite beyond the sinner. And yet, in order for creation to fulfil its purpose, satisfaction must be made, and God alone can bring it about; the term 'must' in this case expressing the character of God's intrinsic, unchangeable honour. Satisfaction for sin, therefore, can be made only by a God-Man, able, by his divinity, to give something worthy of God, yet able, by his humanity, to represent mankind. Salvation and human happiness, Anselm concludes, are possible only through Christ.[10]

This theory is not scriptural in its terms, and is rational – in the sense of seeking reasons – in its thrust. It has been criticized, above all, for being based upon an analogy with Germanic law, and coloured by a feudal notion of the honour owed to an overlord that is – according to Ritschl and those after him – unworthy of God. Yet, though strikingly new, Anselm's theory won rapid and universal acceptance. It became the current view of the later Middle Ages, and the theologians of the Reformation built upon it.

The reason I draw attention to these two ideas – the feudal three orders, and the satisfaction theory of the Atonement – both of which emerged approximately a thousand years ago, is that they offer between them a view of who we humans are (in the year 1000), and a view of God's agency with respect to us. Neither idea came on the stroke of the millennium, nor was either a 'big' idea in the sense of novelty or ingenuity, rather more a phrase or mode of interpretation. But both knew a remarkable and durable success; they served for people at that time to make sense of who they were both with respect to each other and within a horizon of God's action in Jesus Christ. They articulated a convincing 'bottom line', beyond which people did not need to go. And their success in so doing goes a good way to explaining why the dating system of Dionysius Exiguus has persisted for well over a thousand years (a good deal longer than the first millennium), and why therefore planes threatened to fall out of the sky in the year 2000. One might go further, and generalize the point, and say that a system of dating survives because – and as long as – it gives peace and human flourishing. That is why one dates events from the accession of a good king.[11]

The task in hand

The demands of the present situation are broadly similar to those in the year 1000. The task of the thinking classes in general – and for the reason given above (in Chapter 4), the Church has a specific role – is to create an understanding that both draws upon popular perceptions and gives them shape, an interpretation that is at once convincing and offers this freedom, the ability to operate better in the world, an interpretation that helps make sense of things. This interpretation, to repeat, will not be a great intellectual apparatus, but a phrase or two, a condensation of meaning. Nor will it be constructed with a thousand-year prospect in mind: it will respond to the demands and possibilities of the moment, which are great enough. It will give a way of imagining how human power and human will may be articulated in a structure of trust, a series of commitments under God, that might allow human nature, human flourishing and divine order to be joined together. In short, we are seeking an account of social order and a matching account of God's order that together carry conviction, which need to be developed in common through some process of paying attention to the situation in which we find ourselves. These accounts do not yet exist; but I can offer two indications of the dimensions of the problem.

First, I would reiterate how sophisticated is Aldabero's settlement. He suggests three things: the separation of the different social orders, the hierarchy – though with possibilities of reversal – between these orders, and nevertheless their interdependence: they can exist only together. All this lies within an understanding of a Trinitarian God, whose work for the salvation of humankind in Jesus Christ can then be articulated in appropriate terms. On the other hand, our contemporary common-sense categories – although we maintain the reality of the spiritual, political and economic spheres – holds little brief for difference, less for relations of authority and duty, and almost none for interdependence: we have no public account of life in common. At the same time, the commonest understanding of the work of God in Christ is essentially individualistic: the appeal of Christ to every sinner.

Second, I would suggest that our situation in broad terms might be thought of usefully less as being post-modern than as pre-modern: what is in danger of breaking down is the seventeenth-century settlement whereby people in Western Europe decided that, after three generations of religious wars, political agreement and peace were more important, more central to human flourishing, than making religious truth prevail. And the Church of England is a Christian consecration of that political settlement, which did not abandon criteria of difference, rights and duties, and their interdependence. In the present situation, it is confronted with both an opportunity to renew that vocation and, the other side to that challenge, a threat.

The task, as I conceive it, therefore has a strongly Anglican flavour. The Prayer Book on the one hand summons us to 'make prayers and supplications, and to give thanks, for all men'; that is, we have a particular task with respect to the whole (be it at parish or national level) that does not wait upon universal recognition; and on the other, it suggests an outcome, to live 'in love and charity with your neighbours'; that is, it reflects upon the state of the polity. What I am suggesting is in line with this conception of the Church's identity and role; it is worth noting that other churches will have different and distinct vocations with respect to the Millennium.

In brief, and in sum: the new millennium, for good reasons, had some disturbing qualities. We might put it in this way: while we seek pleasure, wealth and even salvation in largely individualistic modes, we increasingly share risks and uncertainties collectively. The task is to respond to that disturbance by once again articulating a social vision of human flourishing, within a theological vision of who God is and what he has done for us.

9

Giving

———•◆•———

In most public services, a collection is taken, and I want to consider the question, why? I would add immediately that it is not my purpose to incite people to give more; I am, rather, interested in the significance of the fact. We might put the problem like this: it is curious that collections occur in almost every church service, and yet it is not the case that all aspects of the management and mechanics of running a church and a congregation are represented in the liturgy. So why does money feature?

The cathedral represents one end of a spectrum. My job is in a Cambridge college chapel, at the opposite end of the spectrum in vastness of responsibility, and the collection there is taken discreetly, generally only mentioned obliquely, and distributed in its entirety to a number of charities, chosen for their worthwhileness. The chapel is wonderfully independent of financial burdens; we do not have to worry directly about raising money for restoration, maintenance and so forth, and the discretion as to money is perhaps the counterpoint to that. But in the majority of places of worship, in most churches, where finance has to be a constant theme, collections are focused upon, and a whole theology of giving and covenanting, stewardship and tithes enunciated. Both positions, discreet or prominent, reflect the needs and demands of the situation, and I'm not sure either gets to the bottom of why we have collections, why money obtrudes into the service.

The basic discussion of such matters in the New Testament occurs in Paul's second letter to the Corinthians, where he raised the question of a collection for the church in Jerusalem. We tend to think of this collection as honouring the founding congregation, paying one's dues, as it were. But, if you pause to think for a moment, it is even rather odd that the source and origin of the faith should show an apparent lack of vigour and need money. One might expect the church in Jerusalem to be a missionary church, in the jargon (it was, of course), providing funds and people to spread the gospel, and correspondingly energetic and well-ordered in its own life. But it was not like that. Because of the Temple, and the associated custom of giving alms, Jerusalem had, apparently, the biggest population of people who lived by begging in the ancient world. Religious sites have this effect: they attract beggars – in large part, because people who go on pilgrimage are more likely to give away money. At home, they are sober citizens who know the value of money, but in these religious places, obligations to charity are writ large, and there are gathered objects of charity to exploit this. Giving to charity, almsgiving, we might note, is a thoroughly ambiguous business. And the problem that confronted the first Christian congregation, in Jerusalem, was that too many of its members came from the begging classes, and rapidly needed support. Hence, once the congregation took on the task of supporting their poor and needy members, the Church as a whole took on a beggarly aspect: it too looked pretty unrespectable and needing help.

It is worth pausing further upon the ambiguities of charity. Considered from the human angle, almsgiving of any kind, including giving to collections, is a thoroughly messy business, shot through with what one might call 'bad faith'. Not only do the recipients frequently seem undeserving, but also, as we have seen with the church in Jerusalem, by associating with them one may become similarly tarnished. What is worse, one's motives for giving are frequently murky: does one do it in order to reward oneself – with good feelings, with the recognition of others, with the sense of duty done, or of good achieved? And does one ever give more than one could afford? What would that mean, especially if salvation were involved?

We try to get round these problems by certain institutional techniques, so, while we may shamefacedly give to the odd beggar, in general we covenant to registered charities, who are accredited by the Charity Commissioners as being well run and deserving. But the underlying ambiguities are not, by that, done away with. And the reason why they are not done away with is that all our reasonings, arguments and so forth, our attempts to balance motivations, needs, outcomes and so on, are attempts at calculation, at balancing the books. Hence we give as much as we can afford, reckon the good we do, estimate the feelings mobilized, the ends achieved, even the salvation gained.

Now, how does Paul argue for his collection for the church in Jerusalem? He does not offer any moral pleading, that one should give, that it is a good cause, and so forth; in brief, he does not calculate. Rather, he says God gave everything for a set of people without either merit or hope, without any good reason other than his character, or who he is. And giving is how you join in with his character and action and purposes for the world.

Money is of course ambiguous: it is one of the principal sources of our earthly desires, it moves us, and it shares in our profound ambiguity, whether as donors or recipients. But, by grace, it may also be the means of grace, by which our collective lives are transformed into the life of Christ, by which the New Adam is born out of the Old. This new life erupts in the material of the old, so that giving generously, rather than calculating the odds, becomes a human possibility. God has acted in Christ, so it is possible for us to give generously.

One should note that giving will be painful, just as God works through Christ crucified. For it is not natural to give away money: money is in some respects the lifeblood of the Old Adam. That is its significance, but that is also why it can be a source of joy. Listen to how Paul describes to the Corinthians the charity of the Macedonian Christians:

> We want you to know, brethren, about the grace of God which has been shown in the Churches in Macedonia, for in a severe test of affliction, their abundance of joy and their extreme poverty have overflowed in a wealth of liberality on their part. For they gave according to their means, as I can testify, and beyond their means, of their own free will, begging us earnestly for the favour of taking part in the relief of the saints [in Jerusalem] – and this, not as we [Paul and Titus] expected, but first they gave themselves to the Lord and to us by the will of God . . . (2 Corinthians 8.1–5)

The Macedonians have seen the giving of money as a means of participation in grace. Paul expands the theme in these well-known words: 'For you know the grace of our Lord Jesus Christ, that though he was rich, yet for your sake he became poor, so that by his poverty you might become rich' (2 Corinthians 8.9).

We should note that this giving of money is not simply the dissemination of money, its dispersal. Wealthy men in the ancient world drew attention to their honour by having servants throw money to the crowds of paupers. Here there is a reciprocity of recognition. But for Paul, the giving of money contributes to the building of the unity of the body of Christ, and the praise that the recipients give God is part of that unity, from which we all benefit. Because we are transformed by grace, we give; others experience our gift as transforming, and themselves offer up praise, which in turn is experienced as grace for us. As Paul says: 'I do not mean that others should be eased and you burdened, but that as a matter of equality your abundance at the present time should supply their want, so that their abundance may supply your want, that there may be equality' (2 Corinthians 8.13f.).

This is not a balancing of contribution and cost, an economy of calculation, but a matter of generosity, an economy of gift, whereby participation is a blessing for all, and recipients may benefit no less than givers. Indeed, it is hard to sort out who gives and who receives in Christ, once the pattern is begun.

Two comments, and then a brief concluding remark. First, this notion of participation in grace contributing to the unity of the body of Christ actually explains something of how we decide where the money collected goes, the uses to which it is put. If the recipients — however dubious, in human terms — praise God (that is, it helps them to flourish), the givers — however shifty — share in that blessing. Second, this gives some way of grasping what underlies the debates about the remission of world debt and the Jubilee. It is not simply a matter of calculation: the prime fact is that the life of the New Adam is a new sociability, a solidarity founded upon generosity, or grace.

So, to return to the simple question with which I began — why do we have collections in the course of worship? — it is not primarily for good works, nor for supporting worthwhile projects, nor even for the building up of the unity of Christian believers (although the latter is very close to the mark); it is so that we have a mundane means of participating in grace, of imitating Christ, and of joining in the life of Christ, the new sociability founded upon generosity, not calculation.

Through the grace of Christ all of life, including money — with all its power and associated compulsions and dubious motivations — may be transformed and put to work for salvation: brought to share in the blessing of God.

10

Living in the Promised Land

Introductory remarks

In discussing the work done in the Daily Offices, the reading of Scripture in the context of worship takes the central role. As part of elaborating that process, the lectionary used at daily Morning Prayer in the chapel of Jesus College, Cambridge has been drawn up so as to allow an undergraduate to read all of the New Testament and most of the Old in three years of term-time. Nothing is omitted. This placing of Scripture at the centre raises with some urgency the issue of how are those involved to understand what they read: how to form practices of reading and principles of interpretation which will in due time allow the readers of Scripture to show its workings in their lives. These stages correspond to the traditional trio of reading, interpretation and application; they are not easily achieved. In the context of the chapel, therefore, I have worked steadily upon the exposition of Scripture, with the aim of discerning an appropriate approach. The two examples I include – this chapter, summarizing lessons gained in a series of sermons concerning the book of Judges, and Chapter 12, on the beginning of Ecclesiastes – represent the attempt to create and share a non-expert – though educated – engagement with Scripture. They indicate the kind of work I believe to be necessary, referred to in passing in other pieces in this volume.

Analogies

I am concerned with looking in Scripture for sources by which we might understand our own situation. It seems to me that we have to relearn how to read Scripture as the Word of God, so that it is the power in our lives whereby we are renewed and put to work in the world. This is not simple. It is relatively easy to identify one's own strong feelings with a revelation of the mind of God, whether those feelings be aesthetic – inspired by nature – or political – the demand for justice – or, indeed, biblical – when one identifies passages that support one's positions. In every case, it is impossible to discern whether the revelation arises from God or from ourselves. The reason we need to relearn to read Scripture is that one of the marks of revelation is that it alters and changes us as well as confirming and comforting us. The mind of God is not our mind, and it will disturb us. There is no more sure source where we can encounter the mind of God than Scripture – although it is not the only source – and that is where we should start.

Part of that process of being changed is contained in the matter of how we encounter the mind of God, or, to put it another way, not so much reading Scripture as 'being read by Scripture': construed by the mind of God, which, as I have suggested, cannot be separated from the context of worship. However, I am not concerned with this angle here, but rather with how we read and interpret and apply Scripture. That is, beyond reading Scripture regularly in the context of worship, in the conviction that it contains God's mind for us, and exposing ourselves to its power, there is the issue of how we read it and understand it. These, again, are not simple matters, but they can be discussed; it is not a matter of magic. We do not simply read and hope; we read and work and hope. (I may add, there is more still, because there are questions of how we come to a common mind upon what we find when revelation reads us: but that too is not our business now.) What I propose here is one small part of this business of reading and interpreting; I am going to try to find an analogy that may allow us to identify a part of Scripture that in particular speaks to us. So we are looking at analogies that the Bible offers us, or at particular models.

There are various parts of the Old Testament that allow us to identify our situation as a Christian church in different ways. We can think of ourselves as on a journey through the wilderness, for example, or as being in exile, or as living in an occupied country, under an alien empire. These are useful models; they allow us to interpret the world through scriptural understandings, and to begin to search for what the will of God might be in these conditions.

The interest of the book of Judges lies in the fact that it offers us a different model. It speaks about living in the Promised Land, when Israel is neither master nor slave, and where the uneasy balance of power between Israel and the indigenous peoples – the peoples of the land – is conceived in terms of whose way of life will prevail. For the problem for Israel in the Promised Land is that the indigenous peoples' way of life is very attractive; it is simultaneously repulsive and desirable. We will discuss why in due course, but it is in this feature that a possible likeness to our world emerges.

The book of Judges

Let me remind you of the outline of the book. It comes after the oppression in Egypt, and the wandering in the wilderness (in the Pentateuch), and just after the conquest (under Joshua), and comes before the kingdom of Saul (and then David) is set up (in 1 and 2 Samuel). So Judges is set at the period of the conquest and settlement of the Promised Land, before the formation of any sort of political unit, such as a kingdom. That is, in a way, it is the story of Israel before it was Israel – told with hindsight, of course, probably quite a lot later.

So the issues are the *unity* of the tribes of those who follow the Lord God, and also the *purity* of these followers, how they keep themselves apart from the peoples who follow other gods, who already occupy these lands. Effectively, who are the Israelites, and how are they the Israelites? These issues of unity and purity come down in the end to whether they are faithful to the God who has brought them up out of Egypt – or not. As those familiar with the history of the followers of God – or those chosen by him – will know, they are largely unfaithful. And the stories of the Judges, the various leaders of Israel in this anarchistic period, are told in terms of their faithfulness and unfaithfulness, their election, obedience and disobedience, and the consequences of each. The story of Israel is contained in these representatives, raised up by the Lord to save Israel each time they cry out of their oppression to him.

The principal judges are, in order, Othniel, Ehud, Deborah, Gideon (who is followed by Abimelech, who is not a judge), and Jephthah. Then there are various minor judges, before and after Jephthah (Tola, Jair, then Ibzan, Elon and Abdon), and finally, Samson (or in fact, finally, the prophet Samuel, for he was the last of the judges, but he comes in the next book). There are twelve in all, and they correspond to the various tribes. And there is a last part, an appendix, organized around the theme 'In those days Israel had no king; everybody did as he saw fit'.

The issue for us

Overall, the book is undoubtedly unsatisfactory from the perspective of faith, a story of decline, and this focuses the issue for us. For the Promised Land is full of Canaanite pleasures and temptations. Certainly, there is oppression, but more importantly, there is falling away: the Israelites adopt Canaanite ways, and lose memory of Hebrew ways. That is why oppression results. Forgetting, and joining in the indigenous practices, produces oppression, not the other way around. And this parallels our situation and experience: we live in a land of pleasures and temptations, where the issues are, rather than those of exile and oppression, those of joining in indigenous practices and forgetting our Christian calling. And the concluding theme, 'everybody did as he saw fit', has a certain uncomfortably modern ring to it.

The book is in fact constructed around this single question, which is posed in each judge, in whom Israel is identified: does this judge – or Israel – put Canaanite symbols and practices to work in the service of the God of the Hebrews? Or, contrariwise, do the Canaanite symbols take over, and put Israel to work?

The answer is, the story starts well but then goes wrong, as we follow the sequence through. Othniel is a hero. Ehud is a rather dubious trickster, who uses human cleverness to defend Israel. Deborah has Canaanite markings – and Jael, the murderer of Sisera and so saviour of Israel, even more so – but they serve godly ends. Gideon, though a hero, is hesitant, ignorant of his faith and, indeed, from a family that has taken up Baal worship (he destroys the family altar). He represents the turning point of the sequence. His successor, Abimelech, is simply wicked, and a destroyer of Israelites. Jephthah, though an honourable man, knows so little of his faith that he sacrifices his own daughter and descent to honour an oath, child sacrifice being a local indigenous practice. The minor judges are little discussed. And Samson mixes with Philistines and takes on such Canaanite properties as lust, deceitfulness and revenge; he returns ill for ill.

This dismal sequence, I repeat, offers us an account of the world that we might recognize by analogy with our own. The situation is what we might call systematic failure: that is, everywhere one might look for resources to reform and renew the business of following God is already rotten. And the rot comes from the fact that people are not so much oppressed as seduced, drawn to the attractions of the world in which they find themselves. And when crisis strikes, they have few religious resources, for they have forgotten them. How might we escape from this situation?

Resources

The book of Judges, read in this light, is highly organized, and its message, though discouraging at one level, at another contains the source of our hope. For although Israel's leaders are increasingly eaten up by Canaanite symbols and practices, nevertheless God's purposes are not because of that defeated, and these unworthy leaders serve him, and through them, Israel is saved and continued. God's vocation and salvation are extended through these eclipses and errors. Our resource is not human faithfulness, but only the faithfulness of God. That is the lesson of the book, and so in order to understand our own resources, we need to consider what is the nature of the God of Israel that we find in Judges. What is God like, so that we can find hope? This is the central issue, and brings us to the central part of this investigation.

The kind of God we find

In order to answer that, we need to go back to the first chapter of Judges. It begins with a curious pair of stories, stories which compare and contrast the Canaanite gods – the gods of the land – and the Hebrews' God.

The first story concerns a Canaanite king, Adoni-bezek by name, whom the tribe of Judah defeat, pursue, capture and mutilate. (This is the conquest of the Promised Land.) And Adoni-bezek says, 'Seventy kings with their thumbs and their great toes cut off used to pick up scraps under my table; as I have done, so God has requited me' (Judges 1.7). This is a king who serves the Canaanite gods, who dole out measure for measure. They are gods who at best (or at worst) deal in equivalence – what you do to others is in due course done to you. This is a world ordered by power and revenge, and its structure and time are cyclical. Such regularities as it manifests are repetitions of the same.

In cyclical time, you cannot in the end hope for any improvement. The seasons pass, spring is clearly better than winter, but after summer the autumn returns. Similarly, in your youth, you may establish yourself by your guile and your force, and bring down other kings, but you will be served in the same fashion in your turn. It is not that the world is without a certain regularity, and indeed, justice of a kind; nor is it without a certain fertility in due season; but the truth of it all is the rule of equivalence, repetition and circularity. Essentially, do as you would be done by, or, what you put in is what you get out.

The other story in the first chapter of the book of Judges presents a different view of time, and it concerns a Hebrew leader (known to us from the book of Joshua), Caleb, who offers his daughter, Achsah, as wife to whoever can take the town of Debir. A hero, Othniel, succeeds, and is married to Achsah. Othniel becomes the first judge, but we are concerned here with Achsah who, upon her marriage, asks her father for a gift of land, in the Negeb, and also a gift of springs of water, so that the land will be fertile. In the figure of Achsah a number of themes are concentrated: of claiming God's promise of the land and occupying it as a blessing, a blessing in which land and fertility of crops and marriage are all combined. In this story, the new occupants of the land flourish, they are fed and they have descendants. That is, they do not get out what they put in, but get far more, far beyond their deserts: they are blessed.

This is a very different prospect to that offered by the god of Adoni-bezek, where fertility and power, repetition and equivalence were the rule: here we have flourishing, blessing and growth. Indeed, generosity as opposed to equivalence is perhaps the key to grasping what is at stake: blessing instead of measure for measure – and so, it is claimed, time is truly not cyclical, but leads somewhere; it develops, and does not simply repeat.

Elaboration

But the contrast is not a simple one. This is because the blessing is not simply a fiat, the utterance of a power, so the followers of the Hebrew God set out to wipe out the followers of the Canaanite gods. Rather, blessing involves obedience to God, or participation: that is, the follow-ers of God are called to manifest the character of time, its hope and its generosity; God's 'loving-kindness' is the term used. Being blessed involves participation: the business of showing that blessing to others. This poses a dilemma for the Israelites; they cannot simply be a tribe like other tribes, although there is a good deal of debate in this book about genocide and the enforcement of boundaries. Their relation to others is different; they have a calling, to manifest the character of God (and not of man). There are parallels for us.

As we know, the followers of God by and large failed to participate in that blessing. Largely, in the book of Judges, they take to worship-ping Canaanite gods, Baals and Ashteroths (not to mention taking up nasty local practices), and so they tend to go round in circles (and to encounter God's character as righteousness and judgement quite as much as loving-kindness).

But the experience of this human failure simply confirms what they had glimpsed of God's character, and his promise – or the fact that he will not be put off. The book of Judges through its various stories witnesses that the truth of time is generous, rather than repetitious or circular. That is to say, even the repetitions of time are based in the nature of the blessing of God, and human flourishing is, as it were, a deeper truth than measure for measure. This is the lesson of the book of Judges: time, in a word, is worth measuring; it has value, it comes to something. And this is an insight, a claim, worked out in its first forms three thou-sand three hundred years ago, or thereabouts, and transmitted, reflected upon and recorded. And what does time come to? The answer to that is Jesus Christ, but I will only touch on that at the end. Though – a footnote – the death of Christ may be understood as the final transfor-mation of the indigenous practice of child sacrifice; this is putting the ultimate Canaanite symbol – of short-term gain against longer-term benefit (descent) – to work in the service of the Hebrew God.

How does this work out in practice? (Application)

From the start of the book of Judges, two possible ways are sketched out. On the one hand, there is Canaanite religion, with its gods of equivalence: as you do, so it will be done to you. Although this approach contains a certain justice – an eye for an eye – and a certain morality – one of prudence – it is very limited. It lends itself to the view that there is no common good, but only what we might call individual honour – and so it reflects a world that is dominated by human power, and by revenge, as each person seeks to establish their honour, their status, their own private good. The gods of this world were supposed to offer success, and an aspect of this success would be fertility: fertility of crops, and fertility of women. One might note that in this account human sexuality and the productivity of crops and political power are all linked together. And in this account, hope is what might be called short-term, for even if one hopes for – and achieves – power and wives and many herds, the rule of equivalence will come into play, and in due course, in the longer term, you will lose these gains, and be displaced. Note that time is cyclical, hope is short-term, and, although there are clearly individuals, in the sense of named kings, rulers, robbers and so forth, there are no persons, in the sense of historical particularity and development. Each figure is a myth, or an archetype, not a moral actor. This is a different world, but it has a lot in common with our own (calculation, equivalence or exchange, sex as a function of power, stereotypes, circles of time or repetition . . .).

On the other hand, there are the claims of Israelite religion. The basic claim is that God is not concerned with equivalence, but with blessing. And this claim contains within it a different account of justice and of morality, of politics and of time, of sexuality and of personality, of the potential of nature and of hope. For example, we know that in Achsah, fertility – of crops and children – is transformed to flourishing, so that in her is promised that the Israelites will have descendants, and that they will occupy the land, which will feed them, so that instead of equivalence, there is generosity. Time then comes to something, it develops, instead of going in cycles – and it does so because, it is claimed, there is a public good possible, not simply individual honour. Further, as people can join in the good, politics becomes different, because a common well-being is its aim, not the gaining of power (nor the avenging of its loss), and so does sexuality, because it is not an object or means of power, but a means of flourishing. And once time has a shape, people become moral actors, and their decisions matter, and they leave a trace – so the Old Testament is full of accounts of persons, and the actions they take, and the meaning of those actions. If there is a public good, and a story to be joined into, hope becomes real – and the relations of humans to one another, political, familial and sexual, are transformed, as are human relations to nature.

Moreover, we have to develop new ideas of justice, as well as a new morality. And here we begin to encounter a genuine difficulty, which I have already hinted at. For if the truth about the world is that it is based upon generosity, not upon equivalence – and that equivalence is somehow secondary to, and contained within, generosity – then the Israelite God is not simply a tribal god, backing flourishing for the Israelites. Rather, he is the God for all peoples, including the indigenous peoples of the land, with all their nasty gods and practices. Just as the possibility of equivalence, which denies generosity, is contained within generosity, so – the logic is – Israel's God is the one true God, and permits these beliefs and practices that appear to deny him and his uniqueness.

So monotheism, the claim that there is only one God, comes not from tribal rivalry, the boast that our God will destroy your gods. Rather, it comes from the understanding of God as blessing, a blessing which goes beyond each boundary and so, in the end, is concerned with everything, for nothing is exempt from this blessing. This gives a new perspective on the summary of the Law, found in Deuteronomy (6.4) and employed in the Communion Service (in the form from Mark 12.29f.): 'Hear, O Israel, the Lord our God is the only Lord. You shall love the Lord your God with all your heart, with all your soul, with all your mind, and with all your strength'. It claims the reality of blessing, that generosity is what allows the world to make sense, or be intelligible. So before concluding, I want to touch on questions of evidence.

Evidence

Although this paradox can be handled at a logical level – God is the possibility of that which appears to deny him – at a practical level, the puzzle poses all sorts of problems. For if you take the world from a human, flat point of view, the question is, which account of reality is true? Is the basic truth of the world generosity or equivalence?

Because, at a practical level, both accounts have confirmatory evidence. The only means of testing a way is to participate in it: to take up the ways of power, and revenge, and fertility, for example, and see how these ways deliver the goods. Moreover, the Canaanite way delivers its goods speedily: personal honour can be achieved, with skill and good fortune.

Only in due course does the cyclic effect come into play, and there is always the sneaking hope that one might escape the cycle: that one might serve the gods of equivalence and calculation, but that generosity might be one's lot, though it would probably be called luck.

The other way about, to act as if there were a public good, to make clear that blessing is a real possibility, and to act in this faith, will not produce such immediate rewards. The blessing of God, even though real, can only be glimpsed. And this is for two reasons. First, there is an awful lot of self-interest, of seeking personal honour, in the world. And second, because of the nature of blessing, its generosity, the task is not simply to crush the local peoples, to eliminate them, but rather to incorporate them, and put them and their symbols to work for blessing. The blessing of Israel's God is a blessing ultimately for the Canaanites too; the task for the Israelites was to take Canaanite practices and turn them to God's ways. This is a very complex business. And this is very close to the truth of our calling: our salvation and well-being is tied up in ways that need to be explored with the flourishing of the society – and the world – around us.

Summary and conclusion

Let me try and offer a summary, and then a conclusion. Four points:

First, the God revealed in the book of Judges is a God of blessing, and he is followed through faith and participation. In other words, we experience a self-denying generosity as the organizing principle of life, and by sharing in that generosity we become evidence for the truth of such a God. That was true for the Israelites then, and it is true for us now.

Second, the world will both deny this faith and affirm it. The world appears to work by calculation, equivalence and self-interest, but nevertheless it responds to the truth that blessing, generosity and service of others is a deeper reality. That too seems to have been true then and is true now.

Third, by and large, we fail in our calling, by continually being drawn to notions of self-interest, calculation and pleasure, and denying the idea that blessing is the fundamental way that the world works. But that is not the end of the matter, because God's character as blessing means the continual renewal of his projects and purposes. He is not defeated by our incapacities, nor is his character altered by these incapacities. He remains constant, and we experience him differently according to our momentary dispositions or orientations; with the grain, we might say, as loving-kindness, and against the grain, as judgement.

Fourth, and last, part of the point of reading Scripture in the context of worship is to learn collectively how to interpret our experience as the activity of God, so that we learn to read events and trends in the light of his character, as the God of blessing. We learn to live our biblical faith as we learn to be the new Israel, called and blessed by God.

A last point to conclude with. In this book in the heart of the Old Testament, we find the same God that we find in the New Testament. This, I must confess, was a surprise, even a shock, to me. This is our God: a God whose nature is self-giving blessing, who is encountered in the things that deny him, and who demands of his followers that they share in his character – and so, in the end, are called to become a blessing even to their enemies. This is the God who reveals himself fully in Jesus Christ, at work in the people of Israel long ago, before they became a nation.

11

Sacred time

———◦•◦———

My brief is to address the topic of 'sacred time'. In the *Tempus* Exhibition, there is an extraordinary array of things, cleverly conceived and beautifully made, that measure time and its passing. The question that focusing upon 'sacred time' raises is, essentially, why is time worth measuring? What is its interest? This moves us back a stage, from how to measure to why measure, and so to the questions behind the questions – which is one way of describing what is called 'metaphysics'.

The way I will approach the topic is to outline the various kinds of time that are to be found in the Bible, and to draw attention to what I call their 'logic': how they work, and some of their implications. I will try and indicate, albeit briefly, how some of these ideas and implications have found their way into pictures.

Old Testament accounts

We can begin with two juxtaposed accounts from the Old Testament, from the beginning of the book of Judges.[1] This is a book that deals in the conquest of the Promised Land, approximately twelve or thirteen hundred years BC, and so three thousand three hundred years ago, well before the establishment of a Kingdom of Israel, and so prior to any political unit that might wish to measure its own time. The first story – the story of the king Adoni-bezek – concerns the Canaanite gods, gods who deal in equivalence and dole out measure for measure, so that what you do to others is in due course done to you. The world they rule is ordered by power and revenge, and its structure and time are cyclical. The regularities it displays are repetitions of the same; in such a world, you cannot hope for any lasting improvement. This world possesses a certain order and, indeed, a certain kind of justice, but its truth is expressed in the rule of equivalence, repetition and circularity.

The matching story in the first chapter of the book of Judges presents a quite different view of the nature of time, and it concerns the figure of Acsah, daughter of Caleb and wife of Othniel, in whom a number of themes come together, of claiming as a blessing God's promise of the land and occupying it as such, a blessing in which land and fertility of crops and marriage are all combined. In this story, the new occupants of the land flourish, they are fed and they multiply descendants. This is a different prospect to that offered by the god of Adoni-bezek, where fertility and power, repetition and equivalence were the rule: here we have flourishing, blessing and growth. Indeed, the key to grasping what is at stake is to say that generosity as opposed to equivalence is the basis of what is humanly possible: blessing instead of measure for measure – and so, it is claimed, time is truly not cyclical, but leads somewhere; it develops, and does not simply repeat.

We do in fact have a representation of the clash of these two principles, in François de Nome's painting of *King Asa of Judah Destroying the Statue of Priapus* (drawing upon a later account of the conflict, from 1 Kings 15.11–15). But the contrast is not a simple one, and this is because the blessing is not simply opposed to equivalence, each serving as a rival emblem of a competing religion, but instead involves obedience to God, or participation: that is, the followers of God were called to manifest the character of time, its hope and its generosity – God's 'loving-kindness' is the term used. By and large, as those familiar with the Old Testament will know, the followers of God failed to do so. Largely, in the book of Judges, they took to worshipping Canaanite gods, Baals and Ashteroths, and so they tended to enter into cycles of time, and to repeat their errors. But the claim developed, put in terms of God's character and his promise, or the fact that he will not be put off, that the truth of time is generous – coming to something – rather than repetitious or circular. That is, the repetitions of time are based in the nature of the blessing of God, and human flourishing is a deeper truth than measure for measure. Time is therefore worth measuring: it has value – and this is an insight, a claim, worked out in its first form in these accounts of Israel before its formation.

The Jews developed this view of time, that somehow time had to do with humans and their well-being, in two directions. On the one hand, they developed a notion of creation, when order was imposed upon chaos – and so materiality took on the imprint of blessing. And on the other hand, they developed the notion of an End, when the gap experienced between the potential for blessing and actuality would be eliminated: when God would make it clear to all that he was God, and all of creation would live in the fullness of that blessing. So matter and history become the crucial medium for all meaning and value: everything we know lies within the sphere of matter and time, between the moments of creation and the Eschaton, as the End is called. As far as God is concerned, there is of course 'before' creation and 'after' the End – except 'before' and 'after' are not the right words, because they are temporal, and therefore apply to history – but they are not our concern. When asked what God did before creation, Luther replied that he spent his time cutting sticks with which to beat people who asked foolish questions.

You might notice this view of time is not only unlike Canaanite or pagan time, it is also very un-Greek. The Greeks tended to think that time was cyclical, and that the material world concerns a set of repetitions, into which you could be born many times. But the aim was to get out of the material world, and time, to contemplate and participate in the Eternal, the really real, which is neither material nor temporal. Various Renaissance pictures taking up classical themes evoke this view. Cupid and Venus, for example, are mythical figures, outside time – though of course they also generate the endless cycles and repetitions of love and reproduction that we mortals are caught up in. Some Eastern religions have a similar feel. The Jewish point of view is quite different: it is that creation is good, the material is good, time is real (and all you get: no reincarnation), and it comes to something – indeed, it comes to Paradise, the kingdom of God. It is a singular evaluation of time and its potential.

We have in the Old Testament, therefore, what are effectively historical accounts; they are certainly more than mythical. Even the patriarchs – Abraham, Isaac, Jacob – represent not archetypes, but real persons, and real encounters with God, with real consequences: what we might call a logic of historical specificity. The only painting in the *Tempus* Exhibition depicting a patriarch, Castiglione's picture of *Abraham Journeying into the Land of Canaan*, depicted a specific, one-off event, featuring a particular person, not a myth. But the really detailed accounts, concerning human motivations and actions, and their intermeshed consequences, are to be found in the stories of David's court and, after him, of Solomon's empire. Once time gets a shape, other than cyclical repetition, and becomes the medium for meaning, persons and their behaviour become significant in quite a new way.

On the other hand – and, as the saying goes, passing over a great deal of material which would support my case – the glory of Solomon's empire did not endure, and the country was first divided into two kingdoms, and then conquered. First, the Northern Kingdom, Israel, fell to foreign invaders; then, after a long period of wars, so did the Southern Kingdom, Judah, and Jerusalem was laid waste. There followed the Exile – during which period much of the thinking about time that I have been recounting was formulated clearly, and refined. And after the Exile came the Restoration, with the rebuilding of Jerusalem and its walls, and the construction of the Second Temple; but always now under a sequence of foreign rulers. It is not surprising that the Jews, pondering their history, and the nature of time, and their view that creation was basically good, longed for God to bring out this truth about time: for him to make his character and purposes clear. So they began to look for God's Messiah, his anointed or chosen one, in whom the nature and meaning of time would be clarified.

New Testament developments

It was in this context of expectation that Jesus was born, grew up, and began his ministry. He taught, healed the sick, drove out demons, and gathered disciples; and his disciples began to think that he was the Messiah, the Christ: God's messenger, chosen to bring in the kingdom of God. They were confounded, and their hopes dashed, because the occupying authorities, the Romans, in conjunction with the Jewish leaders, arrested Jesus, tried him and executed him. But their hopes were restored, curiously transformed, by the resurrection, which is an event we are still trying to make sense of.

But it is an event, in the logic we are discussing. Just as the Old Testament stories, and paintings, concern specific people and particular events, so too do the various New Testament stories depicted in the exhibition. We have, for example, John the Baptist at work in the River Jordan, the adoration of the shepherds, the massacre of the innocents, Jesus summoning Zacchaeus down from the tree, and various episodes from the Passion. They are all historical, and personal, in the sense that has been described. There is, therefore, one more step to go in this exploration.

The New Testament texts are very largely attempts to make sense of the resurrection event. They contain within them a number of ways of understanding who Jesus was and what has happened in him. Some are more complete, or adequate, than others; and some are more 'moral', one might say, and others more 'cosmological' (although that is a dangerously Greek sort of word). Along cosmological lines, the argument goes, if – as the resurrection proclaims – Jesus is indeed God's chosen one, in whom his character and purposes are made clear and fulfilled, then he is God for us embodied in matter and time. You would not have thought, if you were a Greek, that God could have anything to do with matter and time. And although you would if you were a Jew, you would not think that God would have anything to do with a person who died on the gallows. But this is the claim: that in Jesus, matter and history express fully God's will and purposes. It is an astonishing thing that matter and history could fully express God's will and purposes but, the argument goes, this is what has happened, and therefore Jesus Christ is the key to the meaning of all matter and history: to what it is there for, from the beginning, and to what it will come to, in the End. So, in the New Testament, Jesus is called, among other titles, the Alpha and the Omega, the beginning and the end. And he is also called the Word, or Logos, which means the pattern or reason of things: how they come into being, what they are for, and how they will in the end add up.

But if Jesus, in his birth, life, death and resurrection, is the key, the pattern of all things which ever have been, which are, and which ever will be, he is the centre of time. Our current system of dating (which is itself of fairly recent origin, dating from the late seventeenth / early eighteenth century), which divides time up into time before Christ, numbering down to his birth, and time after Christ, numbering up in the years of Our Lord, is essentially true to the New Testament understanding. Time continues to run between creation and the Eschaton, as it had come to do in the Old Testament, but now we know the centre of time. The key to the pattern of creation, and that in which all creation will be brought together and handed over to God the Father, is Jesus Christ. These aspects are developed, on the one hand, in the first verses of John's Gospel, which discusses how the Word was there, in the beginning, with God and was God – there, therefore, even before creation, in that non-time we cannot usefully talk about – and how all things that are, were made through him, and how he came into the world. And, on the other hand, Paul offers the classic discussions, in Colossians, Ephesians and 1 Corinthians, of how all things shall come together in Christ.

So when you are confronted with a picture of the Virgin and child, or with Tintoretto's *Adoration of the Shepherds*, the construction and perspective are not used simply to focus attention upon the child at the middle of the canvas, but also serve to symbolize the claim that this child is the 'middle' of time. He is how time is, and how it makes sense, and how it comes to something: the pivot of time and meaning, the possibility of history.

The claims of biblical time

There is a great deal more that could be said, but I shall stop here, within biblical time, so to speak. Otherwise, we could discuss the re-emergence of Greek ideas – we have already had hints of this – whereby salvation and well-being are removed from the body, and Christ's body, and time. Or we could talk of the ever-present pagan intuition that time is simply cyclical, that regularities are all there is, and that they do not come to much; and that the best we can achieve is a certain dignified pessimism. It is interesting to note, however, that – by and large – we tend to think that we count for something and that we come to something, that persons and history are, in some quite fundamental sense, real. And so we live out, in some version, the claims of biblical time: we tend to subscribe to the School of Achsah, rather than the School of Adoni-bezek, to return to where I began. Time is worth measuring because it comes to something. And we continue to date our 'common era' from the birth of Christ, observing the subsequent claim, that if time has a meaning, it is because Christ is the centre of time.

12

Ecclesiastes, chapters 1—3

Ecclesiastes 1.1–11: 'All is vanity!'

Questions of method

When reading Scripture, our aim is to allow it to question us: to construe it as the mind of God so that, in the end, it reads us, rather than the other way round. This is quite difficult to achieve, not least in a book such as Ecclesiastes. Some of the biblical books, the historical ones in particular, have a narrative structure, a story that carries you along – even if the story itself, it emerges, has a shape that is intended to instruct you. But there is no story as such in Ecclesiastes, even though there are fragments or episodes on which the imagination can work.

For Ecclesiastes is part of what is called 'Wisdom' literature, which offers teaching on how to think about the world – most likely, indeed, instruction offered to young persons who are training up to be officials: clerks, civil servants, counsellors and so forth. Joseph is a model of such a person, an adviser to the great, showing equanimity and good sense in adversity and in good fortune. There are other examples of such literature in the Bible – the book of Proverbs, the Song of Solomon, and the book of Job, as well as various Psalms – which contain what we might call ordered reflection upon the world and its intelligibility.

The basic material of this literature is often quite crude: folk proverbs and sometimes court sayings. But these are organized and structured. It says in the epilogue at the end of Ecclesiastes, 'Besides being wise, the Preacher [the author] also taught the people knowledge, weighing and studying and arranging proverbs with great care' (12.9). There is an order to this thought.

This presents a problem for us, and it is a problem for all our reading of Scripture: even if written down, the books of Scripture were taught by word of mouth, and the apprentices would be instructed how to interpret. Essentially, one would learn the texts by heart, and then one would be told how to make sense of them, what their significance was. But we lack this second part; we have the collections, but not the instructions or commentaries.

In our own written texts, we try to include 'instructions for use', because we imagine readers utterly unknown to us, and far away, taking up what we have inscribed. Biblical texts, however, were conceived for face-to-face transmission – more like a series of sermons, indeed.

So we need to supplement the text, and supply – even reconstruct – this frame of interpretation. How can we do this reliably? This is the real challenge of reading the Bible – one that has effectively been conjured away by much contemporary practice, which rushes to apply the Bible without thought about the processes of making sense. This is a delicate area, for everybody should read the Bible, and take from it what they can, and I am in favour of the view that the Spirit guides us in our reading. All that I want to do is offer the principles that have emerged in my attempts to understand Scripture, as it works on me.

I employ three tools or techniques. The first to mention, though the last in practice, is to read monographs and commentaries. These, I find, are necessary, instructive and frustrating in equal proportion. Certainly, they should never be substituted for reading and re-reading the text. But they help us sort out what we are reading – and I shall say nothing that is not said elsewhere, even if I have appropriated it to my own understanding, and therefore to a degree misappropriated it.[1]

Second, I find the column of cross-references in the Bible that attaches to the text extraordinarily useful. These are the kind of references the original pupils would have been instructed in. Scripture is in continual conversation and debate with itself: a writer is making sense of his world in the light of previous revelation, applying it and reinterpreting it.

For this reason, each book can serve as a model for how we ourselves use Scripture. Scripture itself contains a way of reading and applying God's word that takes seriously revelation, tradition and reason, or the force and givenness of God's word, the way that this has been received and understood, and putting to work this gift, as received and transmitted. You have to go on thinking and arguing, comparing notes and doing your best with what you are given, because this is how you participate in the Word, and indeed the mind, of God.

And third, as I have already hinted, the individual books themselves often have a structure, a structure that is both associated with making the book memorable and teachable, and contains a way, or at least clues, to interpret the book. The structure itself can be significant.

In the case of Ecclesiastes, I think there is a structure by which the book is folded back upon itself. The book begins with a statement of the thesis, and then passes through a series of episodes, illustrative and didactic, before reaching the midpoint. Whereupon it goes back over the topics, providing, if not solutions, at least another level of thought concerning them, returning to a conclusion that repeats the initial starting point. The one thing to note is that (at least according to my provisional view), the topics in the second half run in inverse order — that is, the book begins with topics A, B, C, D and then, after the midpoint, reviews them in the order D, C, B, A. So the whole thing is constructed as a circle, and you could in theory begin anywhere and run round it.

This is not very important to our reading of the book, particularly because we shall not get far enough through to consider the various potential repetitions. Nevertheless, I mention the notion to introduce two points.

First, you can see that such a structure might help a person in memorizing the text and its content. It has a teaching purpose. And second, if you read the text as if it were modern or contemporary — to be read straight through — it will be found confusing and confused. For topics are repeated, and occur in a different order, and frequently conflicting things are said about apparently the same topic, and even contradictions uttered. Critics indeed sometimes claim the book is prolix, disordered and contradictory. Why it should in that case have survived for over two thousand years then becomes a mystery. It is a better hypothesis to imagine that there is a mind at work in the text at least equal to our own, even if it is different in its workings. So, although we shall not be much concerned with cycles of reading, we shall give credit to the Preacher and try to seek out the meanings of his apparent paradoxes, rather than attributing them to lack of clarity.

The text: 'All is vanity!'

After all that, I want to consider the theme set out at the beginning of the book. The key text around which the book is arranged is the second verse of chapter 1: 'Vanity of vanities, says the Preacher, vanity of vanities! All is vanity!' This is repeated at the end, in chapter 12: 'Vanity of vanities, says the Preacher; all is vanity' (12.8); this is the final verse apart from the epilogues. And the last verses of chapter 6, which serve as a midpoint or turning, serve to expand the point. So what precisely is 'vanity', around which concept the book is constructed?

There is a danger in our handling of the concept: it is easy enough for a modern reader to adopt a cynical or world-weary pose. 'I have eaten of the fruit of life, and it is tasteless.' There are indeed a number of readings that take the Preacher to be a sceptic, or as doubting the value of all things, or even as an existentialist who, when confronted with the absurdity of life, turns in revolt against it. But it is not helpful to move too quickly to reading this book in contemporary terms. The twentieth century was full of scepticism, cynicism and existentialism, but we might suspend these while exploring the text, in order to search out the nuances of its perspectives and arguments.

Perhaps a better place to start is with one of the Psalms. In Psalm 39 we read the following:

> Lord, let me know my end, and what is the measure of my days; let me know how fleeting my life is! Behold, thou hast made my days a few hands' breadths, and my lifetime is as nothing in thy sight. Surely every man stands as a mere breath! Surely man goes about as a shadow! Surely for nought are they in turmoil; man heaps up, and knows not who will gather! (Psalm 39.4–6)

When the Psalmist says 'every man stands as a mere breath', the word 'breath' is the same word that is translated as 'vanity' in our passage from Ecclesiastes. Indeed, the passage from the Psalm is very close in spirit to the introduction to Ecclesiastes: man is created, it claims; life is put in him, but this endures only for a brief and uncertain period, the duration of which man has no control over. Considered in this light, all that man desires and does – which is also breath – is curiously limited in its consequence: it is simultaneously the best he can do – and is indeed what he was made for – and of little or no lasting significance. 'Breath' then points in a single word to mortality, effort, desire, enjoyment, and also to futility and death.

We might say, then, that we are not served very well by Saint Jerome who, when he translated the Bible into Latin (the Vulgate), translated this word as 'vanitas'. It gives rise to the beautiful rhetoric of 'All is vanity!' but at the same time, this lends itself to a proud despair. And that does justice neither to the Preacher nor to the Psalmist. The latter indeed, having summed up human life in this fashion, continues his meditation: 'And now, Lord, for what do I wait?' To which he replies immediately: 'My hope is in thee' (Psalm 39.7). This is not despair.

The word 'breath' then gives you the plot or the frame in a single word. You can see that you might sum it up by taking a single one of its aspects, and so as tempered wisdom, or melancholy scepticism, or as absurdity. But you need to be able to spot that, at the same time, it is a meditation upon the whole nature of man. And a meditation, moreover, with quite probably a glance back to the second chapter of Genesis, where 'the Lord God formed man of dust from the ground and breathed into his nostrils the breath of life; and man became a living being' (Genesis 2.7).

When reading Ecclesiastes, we are meant to have the beginning of the Bible in mind. For the act of creation, and the Fall, leave us with a number of problems, among which are the following: how to relate to life, and to the knowledge of good and evil; how to formulate a settlement between man and woman; how to construe this life of pleasure, toil and pain that has fallen to the lot of men and women, and the place in it of procreation, on the one hand, and death, on the other.

Moreover, it is the task of Wisdom, or of the wise man, the Preacher, to make sense of these things, and to conclude whether they can ever be made sense of. And not least amongst his duties is the ordering and transmission of this wisdom across generations. The verse following the summary or key we have been considering states: 'A generation goes, and a generation comes, but the earth remains for ever' (Ecclesiastes 1.4).

That is as far as we need go in this section: the book of Ecclesiastes might best be understood as a meditation upon the world as it has been bequeathed to us from the account in Genesis, given focus in the passage from Psalm 39. It is a serious attempt to understand our mortal nature in the light given by the God who created us.

Ecclesiastes 1.1–11: death and desire

This passage serves as an introduction to the entire book. The key word to the description of the world, and the situation it contains, is translated as 'vanity', which more literally means 'breath', and so has come to hold secondary meanings of impermanence, transitoriness, and so, perhaps, futility. 'What does man gain by all the toil at which he toils under the sun?' (1.3), the Preacher begins, a rhetorical question which does not lend itself to a speedy answer. Nevertheless, he begins to sketch out a reply, and his reply is essentially a meditation upon the nature of time, and man's relation to it.

The four verses that follow are structured around the elements of creation: we consider in turn earth, sun, air and water. We are told that generations come and go, but the earth remains. The sun rises and sets. The wind goes round the points of the compass. Waters flow ceaselessly in streams to the sea. This is a very complete, though economical, description. We are transient creatures set in a context of endless repetitions, cycles of which ours are perhaps the least important, or at least of no overwhelming significance, even if they are the most troubled.

This contrast, of troubled human transience set in a cyclical world, poses a problem from the human point of view. And the next verses offer a description of man to match the elements of creation, just as you might expect of a meditation based upon the account of creation. You can read it long in Genesis, or short in Ecclesiastes. Here we are told that man is a creature capable of speech, who sees and hears, and who desires – but who cannot be satisfied. In this creation of cycles, man cannot articulate the sense of it, nor can he achieve satisfaction through what he sees or hears. So the Preacher says, 'All things are full of weariness; a man cannot utter it; the eye is not satisfied with seeing, nor is the ear filled with hearing' (1.8).

And he elaborates the problem of desire, or the dissatisfaction of desire, in terms of time: 'What has been is what will be,' he says, 'and what has been done is what will be done; and there is nothing new under the sun. Is there a thing of which it is said, "See, this is new"?' (1.9–10). We have been created with a desire for novelty within us. That is more or less the definition of desire: we desire what is not the case; it is the mark within us of what is not us, and which is not yet. We want the new. And yet you would have to be a fool to imagine you had been offered something new. But that is what we are all like, for we are constantly moved by desire.

We might remark, in this context, that the book of Ecclesiastes is thought to be late in terms of books of the Bible, despite the references to King Solomon. This is argued on grounds of the language used, and the sophisticated and wealthy society glimpsed in the text. So we can place it in a rather Greek world, where various schools of thought offered what you might call 'therapies of desire', ways of being happy in the world. Some philosophers recommended calming desire, and self-control; others that there is nothing but desire. Some proposed that happiness comes only with extirpating desire, and yet others – in a rather sophisticated move – proposed that desire was a product of the way language worked, and that one might do well to be cagey of any philosopher who offered you a therapy based on words in return for payment. The Preacher largely works with Israel's tradition of wisdom texts and other parts of the Scriptures, but there are some signs of the Greek marketplace of ideas.

It is worth noting, too, that in linking the problem of human desire to time, the Preacher adds a further twist. For having pointed to repetition – there is nothing new under the sun: 'It has been already, in the ages before us' (1.10b) – he then adds in the idea of forgetfulness. He concludes, 'there is no remembrance of former things', putting in for good measure 'nor will there be any remembrance of later things yet to happen among those who come after' (1.11). Now forgetfulness explains why we keep on renewing our desire. Novelty and forgetfulness are closely tied together: something may not be new, but we experience it as such. But it also means we are set in a world where our transitoriness knows no relief, not even the limited respite of being remembered.

So we might conclude that the cyclical form of the book, which I mentioned as a possibility previously, is commensurate with the nature of the problem set before us in this introduction: everything goes in cycles. Along these lines we might say that nothing is of more than limited significance, because in the end, everything comes to the same.

Nevertheless, as we have seen, there are topics of compelling interest to humankind which emerge: pleasure and toil, the life of nature, the nature of desire, death and time, the character of mankind, the problems of knowledge and of justice. Moreover, these are the themes which are studied in the sections of the book that follow. We might say that these are topics which defy or go beyond the simple cycle of equivalence. Despite appearances, we keep having insights – both painful and pleasurable – that prompt us to think beyond the cycles that seem to structure the world.

These insights – or the demands we feel – of course arise from the fact that these verses are a meditation upon creation. Underlying all these cycles and these glimpses of possibility and meaning is the gift of creation, the act of the giver for whom there is no possible or adequate return. The gift of God, his blessing experienced as there being something rather than nothing, is present throughout as the possibility of the paradoxes of being breath, or transient.

In the end, I suspect the highly intelligent (and useful) commentator who likens 'vanity' to 'absurdity', and compares the Preacher's stance before transience to Camus' revolt at the ultimate meaninglessness of the world, is simply wrong. The Preacher is concerned with meditating upon the relation between, on the one hand, God's blessing experienced as creation and, on the other, the equivalences or identities by which we make sense of creation, through which his generosity escapes our perception, except in the form of puzzles and paradoxes. These paradoxes can include the appearance of God's absence from the world, so this attitude is neither pious nor optimistic but it is, we might say, realistic and faithful; the Preacher is both troubled and blessed.

There is one more echo from Genesis, which I think bears out this interpretation. The Preacher is clearly concerned with pondering the lot of humankind, or Adam, as the word is. Adam, as we know, has two sons in Genesis. The elder was called Cain, which means 'possession' or 'acquisition', and the younger brother was called Abel, which is in fact the same word that is translated as 'breath' or 'ephemeral' or 'vanity'. Now, we do not need to make too much of this – and word scholarship, especially in a language (Hebrew) that I do not possess, is thoroughly shaky ground. But these names and their meanings would have been in the Preacher's mind, for he was far more given to using Scripture to think with than we are.

We might suggest that the impermanent younger brother, who entered the story only to die prematurely, murdered by his older brother, serves as a mirror for the history of humankind, in the eyes of the Preacher. But his life was not by that incompleteness made meaningless; for the one thing we know about Abel is that he offered the best of his flock as a sacrifice, and the Lord had regard for him and his offering (Genesis 4.4). We might therefore suspect that in Ecclesiastes, the resolution offered to the fleeting and uncertain nature of life – uncertain in terms of what it means – is that its meaning is: to be found pleasing to God.

And in this respect, Abel is a prototype of our Saviour, for Jesus too lived a life whereby he pleased God, and that led to his execution in the hands of a jealous elder brother (in Christian eyes), the human authorities. This death too we can say was simultaneously meaningless, in the sense of being undeserved and unsatisfactory, and significant, in that it not only has meaning, but also gives meaning.

This I think is then the shape at the heart of the book of Ecclesiastes, contained already in the introduction: a meditation upon human meaning in the light of creation, a meditation that we find resolved in its fullest form in the cross.

Ecclesiastes 1.12—2.11: Solomon's memoir

This passage is taken from a longer section of the book, and takes the form of a memoir, beginning, 'I the Preacher have been king over Israel in Jerusalem' (1.12). This is a testimony attributed to King Solomon – and indeed, the title of the book, its inscription in 1.1, is 'The words of the Preacher, the son of David, king in Jerusalem'.

Now, we know this book is not thought to come from such an early period; scholars come to this conclusion by pointing to the language employed, the social contexts it refers to, and the preoccupations it displays. But Solomon is taken as the figure of a wise man, wise above all others; and in the tradition, this book, the book of Proverbs and the Song of Solomon are all attributed to him. In fact, for what it is worth, some rabbis attributed the Proverbs to Solomon's youth, the Song of Songs to his maturity and Ecclesiastes to his old age, even his senility.

Be that as it may, it was an accepted ancient form to write a memoir as a posthumous statement coming from a prominent person. In it, there would be included a recitation of that hero's accomplishments, a collection of the principles or maxims – often in proverbial form – which had guided this exemplary life, and exhortations to the hearers or readers to reflect upon their own life and death. There is, therefore, no pretence in the Preacher speaking as he does: the author spoke in the name of a great man, and this fact was clear to all.

The general theme of such memoirs is to raise the question, can the dead be happy? Implicit in the form are supplementary questions as the following. Can a life, even such a life, make sense? Does a human life add up to anything and and – another version of that question – what, if anything, survives death? For all its apparent grandeur – the life, the maxims and the lesson of a great man – this is quite an insecure form of meditation. This sense of insecurity is part of the evidence for dating the book rather late. And this is the first time this reflective literary mode appears in the Bible.

This mode, of course, has been adapted, as we would expect, to serve the purposes of faith. It has been adapted in two ways. The first novelty is that it undermines the authority of Solomon. For it takes as its subject a man of great power and supreme insight, and yet the first passage has him say: 'It is an unhappy business that God has given to the sons of men to be busy with. I have seen everything that is done under the sun; and behold, all is vanity [breath] and a striving after wind' (1.13b–14).

I do not want to call this irony. Rather, it renounces the pretension to mastery, to knowing everything and controlling everything. Luther says that this book is Solomon's *Politics*: it advises against arrogance in authority. We might say that renouncing the fantasy of controlling things is a preparation for faith. Indeed, the whole passage may be seen as a compact statement about a series of steps of renunciation that are needed to free oneself from illusion in order to open oneself to God's illumination. It concerns the process of purification and discernment, by which one learns to participate in God's life. So that is the first surprising thing to say about the way the memoir is used: it becomes a manual of spiritual transformation. We shall come back to this point.

The second novelty of the use of the mode is that it appeals to Solomon's own experience. Instead of pointing to various forms of received wisdom, and invoking particularly pertinent parts of the tradition, and saying 'these were enough to guide an exemplary life such as my own', Solomon says, on the contrary, 'this is what I have tried out, and this is what I have found out'. This is important. It is not the end of wisdom, but it is putting wisdom to work, seeing how it makes sense for this time. Notice that, despite the form it is expressed in, it is not a particularly individualistic form of experience, for the Preacher is addressing a group, and seeking to instruct and convince them. After all, he cannot appeal to Solomon's experience as definitive, since he has questioned the acceptance of unreasoned authority: it is, in the end, breath or wind. This is teaching by an appeal to collective reasoning and common conviction.

So we are offered a clear method, within the will of God, concerning 'the unhappy business that God has given to the sons of men to be busy with'. You (in the plural) have to apply tradition, to make sense of what you find, but at the same time, you have to evaluate it against experience, for what you discover recasts how you understand tradition. And this can only be done by comparing notes. In a slogan, we might say 'revelation, tradition and reason'.

Now the basic question structuring this memoir is the relation between effort and reward. Man has been placed in a world where he is forced to work; he works in order to gain pleasure; and whether he succeeds in this aim or whether he fails, he dies. This frame is articulated early in Genesis, and Solomon is an ideal figure to explore its hints and possibilities, for he simultaneously knew more of life's pleasures than any man, and had more wisdom than any other to draw from these pleasures their enduring truth.

The second chapter begins with Solomon setting himself to 'make a test of pleasure' (2.1), endeavouring – with a wise mind – 'to lay hold on folly', to 'see what was good for the sons of men to do under heaven for the few days of their life' (2.3). Yet remark that, although he seems to gesture towards what we might think of as 'mindless' or empty pleasures – laughter and wine – this is not all that he intends. He undertakes a far more serious project, one of creation. For he immediately goes on, 'I made great works' (2.4), and here we have an implicit comparison with God's acts of creation.

This comparison is not surprising, for Solomon built the Temple, and its site was supposed to be on that of the Garden of Eden and, like Eden, it was guarded by the cherubim. The Temple, indeed, was meant to be Eden restored, God's garden.

And the comparison is made pretty explicit, for Solomon's creative acts are sevenfold in form, recalling – this time – the first chapter of Genesis. There is a rhythmic form to verses 4 to 8, hidden by the prose printing in some Bibles, but obvious when these verses are laid out as poetry:

> I made homes | and planted vineyards for myself;
> I made myself gardens and parks | and planted in them all kinds of fruit trees.
> I made myself pools | from which to water the forest of growing trees.
> I bought male and female slaves | and had slaves who were born in my house;
> I also had great possessions of herds and flocks, | more than any who had been before me in Jerusalem.
> I also gathered for myself silver and gold | and the treasures of kings and provinces;
> I got singers, both men and women, | and many concubines, man's delight.

This is a sevenfold act of creation, recalling the seven days of God's creation.

Now, as he created, God pronounced each thing good and, with humanity added, very good. What about Solomon, in the perspective of the Preacher? In contrast, Solomon says: 'Then I considered all that my hands had done and the toil I had spent in doing it, and behold, all was wind [breath] and a striving after wind, and there was nothing to be gained under the sun' (2.11).

This is an astonishing statement, for we are, after all, talking about Jerusalem, the Temple, and the history of Israel, all at their height, in the reign of Solomon. Is this empty? Well, not quite. But the Preacher is making a new claim. Previous thinkers, considering the decline and fall of Israel, the capture of Jerusalem by its enemies and the destruction of the Temple, had attributed these bad things to Israel's lack of faithfulness to their God. The Preacher, without denying this interpretation, is saying that Israel's kingdom, including Solomon's greatness and the Temple to the living God, was bound to be transient because it was a human enterprise. There is one thing we know, and that is that human achievement is ephemeral.

So rather than a comparison, there is a contrast between God's acts of creation and those of Solomon. And this contrast was introduced in the first chapter, as between the timelessness of creation and man's endless repetitions. But in fact, as we saw, the one allows the other: man's creativity is permitted by God's creation. We are offered here the beginning of an understanding of the place of toil and pleasure: they are the expressions in time of man's status as a created being. Man is made unhappy when he aspires to become like God, and desires his works – and his pleasures – to last for ever. The same works and pleasures can be experienced as blessing when he experiences God's creation as a creature, and therefore in faith. The contrast is between restlessness, or the vain aspiration to control time and its works, on the one hand, and assurance, or living faithfully in time, on the other. The one is folly, the other wisdom.

The lesson that Solomon presents to us is one that is well presented by the greatest and wisest of kings: there is nothing but folly in the desire to know all things and rule all things; the beginning of wisdom is in the fear of the Lord. Let us pray to be given grace to live faithfully in the time that has been given to us.

Ecclesiastes 2.9–26

Solomon is at one and the same time the model of a wise man and the model of a king, a man in whom understanding and power come together. He is in this way very much like a human or pagan idea of what a god is like; he both sees further than we do and has far more ability than us to act upon what he sees.

Yet, when Solomon, who is little less than a god, reflects upon all that he has created – upon his kingdom, his wealth, his treasures – he contrasts his creation with that of the true God. For his – Solomon's – achievements are but breath: impermanent, mortal and destined to perish. And in this they are utterly different to the creative acts of God, which endure for ever. So we are instructed in the absolute distance that exists between God's acts and men's actions.

Nevertheless, because he sees clearly, Solomon knows that these human achievements are not without worth, for they are themselves the expressions of God's blessing on us. We are created creatures, who live by God's gift in time. Our mortal creations, our toil and pleasures, are how we experience God's act of creation, which is good. There is a very strong point being made here, concerning the right way of seeing the world and of living in it.

So Solomon points us to the beginning of wisdom, which is to live in the fear of God, recognizing the nature of his gift to us in the paradoxes of time. It is our nature as created creatures to toil, to produce impermanent achievements and to experience passing pleasures, and to die, to be replaced in due course by those who come after us. If we are wise, we learn to live in God's gift and to praise him through our lives. If we are foolish, we wish that we were not created but eternal, like God; that our pleasures lasted for ever, that our achievements were everlasting, and that pain and toil and death were wiped away. You might notice that this folly is a fantasy, a fantasy of control and permanence which is impossible even in its own terms, for without time, the pleasures and achievements would lose all their meaning and savour. On the other hand, faith is the proper and appropriate way of living in time; it contains a relation to the truth, and permits the possibility of what we may call an 'appropriate understanding'.

We should notice, too, that Solomon's teaching makes this appropriate understanding, or wisdom, inescapably bound to time, and to God's action in time upon us. He describes what we can call a pathway of discernment, whereby we gain wisdom in time as we find God or, rather, since we need a motive force other than ourselves, as God finds us. For we begin in illusion and, left to ourselves, we could only repeat these illusions, desiring pleasures, seeking achievements, and wanting them to last for ever. Yet we need to purge ourselves of these illusions, and only as we do so shall we discover new understandings. We are altered as we take part in something that is not ourselves; that is what faith is, the mark in us of what is not us, but God's action in us. And as we take part, we change and gain new possibilities, so that what we remember

and what we know, and what we want, are all recast; we gain a different past, present and future to the ones we would have had, had not
faith wrought its work in us. We are transformed in every part, in ways
that cannot be predicted, but only lived through.

In the previous section, I outlined how the memoir as a literary form
is recast in Ecclesiastes in two ways: first to offer a vehicle for instruction in these processes of discernment, and second to point in this instruction not to tradition but to Solomon's experience. For he too is
altered as his faith and understanding grow. This process is detailed in
the verses we are now concerned with. This is the lesson of Solomon's
developing understanding, as faith transforms him. So let us follow the
lesson through.

Everything, we know, is based in God's gift, in his blessing. This is
the business — unhappy or not — that God has given to the sons of
men to be busy with (1.13). It is on the basis of this understanding that
Solomon can say that 'wisdom excels folly as light excels darkness'
(2.13): wisdom, as we have suggested, begins with the attitude of faith
which grasps that everything lies within God's blessing — and folly is
without that basic insight. It is on this basis that Solomon can claim to
be 'surpassing all who were before me in Jerusalem' (2.9), and that in
the concluding verse of the memoir he can state: 'For to the man who
pleases him God gives wisdom and knowledge and joy' (2.26a). It is
not that he is claiming that every good thing comes to the man who is
wise — we have plenty of textual evidence against that view — but rather
that wisdom is the way of participating in God's nature as blessing.
Wisdom is an expression of God's work in us, just as much as faith is.

And what is fundamental to wisdom is a grasp on the relation of
blessing to what is the case, or of generosity to calculation. For the mark
of created things — if you leave God out — is that this thing can be taken
to be equivalent to that; so much work is worth so much pleasure. But
blessing exceeds any form of equivalence.

For, if you remember, the subject-matter of the memoir is the relationship of toil to pleasure, a review of what can be achieved in a human
life, and an evaluation of its worth. What are we told about effort, and
calculation? I want to draw out two aspects.

First, effort and calculation are needed — they are man's fate — but
they are not sufficient. You cannot by toil guarantee pleasure or success
or joy, nor for that matter knowledge and wisdom. We might say that,
although you are condemned to work, your profit is uncertain. You
may work and not be rewarded; or you may gain a great deal, and die
to leave it to another who has not laboured for it; or you may even be
favoured and gather where you did not sow. There is a careful tabula-
tion of these apparent injustices, where effort and reward do not stack

up. And the Preacher says, strikingly, that the relation between effort and reward is sufficiently irregular for one to come to loathe both toil (2.18) and life (2.17).

Yet he does not stop at this point of loathing and despair. The Preacher's more reasonable conclusion to this survey is that you should expend sufficient effort, but not an excessive amount. Effort, with its implication of calculation – so much work for so much reward – is a necessary means, but a false idol if it becomes the end for which you aim. He says, famously, 'there is nothing better for a man than that he should eat and drink, and find enjoyment in his toil. This also, I saw, is from the hand of God; for apart from him who can eat or who can have enjoyment?' (2.24–5) This is not despair.

We might note that this attitude contains a health warning against the capitalist mind, where endless effort is demanded by the insatiable desire for mastery and possession. This desire can never be fulfilled. This attitude of mind is not, therefore, a recent invention.

The second aspect is this. It is important to grasp that the approach outlined and demonstrated by the Preacher is progressive and takes place in time. I have laboured this point already from one angle; here I want to emphasize that the notion of progression means that different positions are expounded at different points, for the perspective changes. Indeed, reality changes as you are transformed. If we go over the outline of the memoir, it contains three stages.

Initially, God's gift stirs in you, so that you experience desire for the world, and toil to fulfil this desire. You seek to gain and consume pleasures, including wealth, women (if you are Solomon) and wine. This is folly, but God is at the bottom of it; he is both in it and denied by it.

Then, through this experience, wisdom is stirred and you become repelled by folly, tired by work, and sickened by pleasure; you turn to hating life, for it has become grievous to you. As before, God is both in this growing wisdom and not in it. For wisdom itself has to learn its limits: it too is a striving after mastery and possession – possession this time by the mind, rather than by the body. This is quite as far from knowing God as was the first stage. The Preacher emphasizes this equivalence by noting that one fate – death – awaits the wise man and the fool alike: 'Then I said to myself, "What befalls the fool will befall me also; why then have I been so very wise?"' (2.15).

It is only by passing through this second stage that you can learn to accept God's gift, and live in creation and love it without the desire to possess and consume it, either via the body or the mind. Ellen Davis, whom I have been following in much of what I have said, points to the exemplification of this attitude in George Herbert's prayer: 'Teach me, my God and King, in all things thee to see; and what I do in anything, to do it as for thee'. One could follow that hymn further, for it could have been written by the Preacher. The calling of wisdom is to learn to live in the world that God has created, guided by the eyes of faith.

In sum, in this memoir the Preacher is describing the stages of what we may call the purification of desire. Desire is the restlessness that God puts into man so that he can never settle for any particular thing, whereby that thing is identical to the thing that was wanted, so that desire is satisfied. Equivalence cannot satisfy desire. But this restlessness draws man into a participation in God's blessing, which exceeds any equivalence. Desire, we can say, is the mark of God in the created creature, and is expressed in the wise man in two things: in a certain passivity before the world, and in a longing for justice.

This leads to my last point. Because the Preacher is a man being transformed through desire for God, which is an expression of God's desire for him, he resembles other Old Testament figures such as the author of Lamentations and the Man of Sorrows in Isaiah 53. In him the activity of God, which simultaneously loves creation and judges it, is made clear. The pathway each delineates describes the judgement and purging of folly as the other side of the participation through faith in God's blessing: it is a single process of alteration and development.

And therefore the Preacher also prompts us to see in him an anticipation of the figure of Christ, in whom God's way of being in the world and our way of being in God is revealed. We might say that the book of Ecclesiastes, in common with much else of the Old Testament, is thoroughly Trinitarian in nature; it points to the activity of the one true God.

Ecclesiastes 3.1–15

In the view of the Preacher, we are created by God, blessed and gifted by him, and we can take part in his gift but we cannot own it. We are created for a life of toil and pleasure, and this is carried out in time. Time could well be another way of describing the basic dimension of human life; instead of wind or breath, or vanity or ephemerality, we could say all is. temporal.

The task of wisdom is to learn to live well within the limitations and opportunities of this given time. This is by no means a straightforward business, for there is a temporal dimension to understanding and, moreover, its temporality is not linear but recurrent. That is, we do not progress steadily as we see more, each day becoming wiser and wiser. Instead, we recast our grasp on things as we proceed to develop in wisdom, for wisdom itself – like faith – is participation in the mind of God. (Which is why it may be gained, in part, through the reading of Scripture.)

As we proceed, therefore, every aspect of ourselves is changed – not only what we know, but also what we want and what we remember. Our past, present and future are all recast in the process that leads to understanding, so that there can be no simple personal identity preserved throughout. Indeed, as one writer puts it, even our faculties are transformed: knowledge is changed to faith, memory to hope, desire to love, so that rather than living by knowledge, memory and desire, the wise person lives by faith, hope and love. In the perspective of wisdom, we are altered beyond recognition; in the words of one of Paul's letters, we are transformed from glory to glory.

Given all this, you can see that time will be a key idea in any attempt to convey an account of our lives as created beings; it is the key to our identity as we change.

It is therefore unsurprising that, after King Solomon's memoir, in which some of the issues are laid out in a discussion of toil and pleasure and the limits thereof, we find a treatise on time. This treatise begins with a very famous poem, often read at funerals, the first line of which runs: 'For everything there is a season, and a time for every matter under the sun' (3.1). This poem is followed by a discussion. I will look at each part; first, the poem.

The poem makes the claim that there is an adequate and proper time for every necessary element of life. This is a remarkable view of providence. It sets aside any suggestion that life is meaningless and chaotic, any suggestion that it simply consists in a series of events without reason (one damn thing after another), or a series of cycles without resolution.

You might notice, too, that it develops the notion that time is the dimension that God has given us within which to operate, for it claims that life and time are punctuated by events, and that these are somehow appropriate, or fitting. Time consists not so much in duration as in punctuation, and in some sense it is fitted to us.

It almost does not need saying that this is an important claim with respect to how you view your life and its opportunities. And the claim also gives one pause for thought with respect to so-called accidents, calamities, sickness and death. On this view, clearly you do your best – you toil and seek pleasure – but you should not imagine that your failures to achieve mastery and control constitute a defeat, for it is God's time for us that we are dealing in.

Such a perspective is found in the Prayer Book's 'The Visitation of the Sick', where it says: 'Dearly beloved, know this, that Almighty God is the Lord of life and death, and of all things to them pertaining, as youth, strength, health, age, weakness, and sickness. Wherefore, whatsoever your sickness is, know you certainly, that it is God's visitation.' And so forth. There is a whole spirituality (if that is the word I want) contained here, one that is radically God-centred. There is no sense of there being bits of life in which God is involved, and bits in which he is not, no dualism. There is one God and one world, entirely contained within his blessing.

The poem, then, translates this perspective. It first pairs and contrasts a series of physical and emotional elements of the personal life, starting with being born and dying, including loving and hating, and also killing and healing (which I will mention again later). It also contains an inventory of the elements of social existence – war and peace, uprooting and planting, the breaking down of nations and their building up and, probably, economic exchange, denoted by stones cast away and gathered. (There are other interpretations of this last verse, including an erotic one. It is worth remarking that the problems of translation are considerable, and scholars argue in detail about thoroughly incompatible interpretations. One simply has to do one's best: you cannot be put off reading Scripture by the expertise of scholars; it is too precious.)

The poem presents a census of human activities, these activities making concrete the transitoriness of things. Time – God's blessing for us – consists in the realization of particular events. You should notice this is not simple fatalism. There are not, for example, times for oppression or suffering, for deceit or folly. But there is an order made for man – and made for every person – by God. And, as the final verse effectively says, why struggle against it? 'What gain has the worker from his toil?' (3.9) As Solomon's memoir points out, it is wise to join in and take pleasure, but it is folly to put in excessive effort in a fantasy of control.

Before I go on to consider the Preacher's reflections on this account of time, a footnote on the difficult phrase 'a time to kill, and a time to heal' (3.3a). This may be construed as regarding the completeness of the transformation of the person, whereby the old is destroyed, making way for the new. Gregory of Nyssa glosses the phrase with the example of killing the tapeworm of hatred by the medicine of the Gospel, resulting in healing and restoration. This casts a proper light on the concept, and also rebukes crude and literal readings.

What are we to make of these times? In this case, the Preacher offers us a number of conclusions, rather than – as in the case of the memoir – observations from stations along the way.

First of all, he observes (and as we know), that the occupation necessary to human life is God's gift: 'I have seen', he says, 'the business that God has given to the sons of men to be busy with' (3.10). Time is our medium, our situation.

Then he makes a threefold observation. In the first place, everything that happens does so in its appropriate time, for God 'has made everything beautiful in its time' (3.11a). But, secondly, man does not live solely in time, for God 'also has put eternity into man's mind', or, as we might put it, he has made our hearts restless, until they find their rest in him. So we live in time with an aspiration towards that which makes time possible, to that which exceeds time. And further, thirdly, within time, man cannot grasp the order of times, 'so that [man] cannot find out what God has done from the beginning to the end' (3.11b). In short, within this appropriate order of times ordained by God, man can grasp neither the mainspring nor the detail of that order.

All this within a single verse. It follows that man must live humbly, by faith. Just as in Solomon's memoir, the Preacher offers us this conclusion: 'I know that there is nothing better for them than to be happy and enjoy themselves as long as they live; also that it is God's gift to man that everyone should eat and drink and take pleasure in all his toil' (3.12–13).

This point of view is neither sceptical nor melancholy. Much of the remainder of the first half of the book is a more detailed examination of the hard realities such a perspective has to take into account and, indeed, contend with. Here we are simply offered a certain summary of the basic attitude open to created and faithful men and women.

The conclusion contains a summary of this account of time, put rather succinctly, as we have become used to. Let me try to spell it out. The Preacher offers what we might call a strong view of providence: 'I know that whatever God does endures for ever; nothing can be added to it, nor anything taken away' (3.14a). Fair enough, let us reply, but from our human point of view, we cannot understand the purpose of this creation, of these acts. We simply experience this purpose in time sometimes as pleasure, sometimes as pain, always as ephemeral. To what end? And he replies, 'God has made it so, in order that men should fear before him' (3.14b); we can live in this providential order by faith, through worship.

We may then ask, what of the good men do that is forgotten, and of the evil they do that remains unpunished and of the sufferers left un-restored? How does one live faithfully in time, since eternity has been put into our minds, without giving way to cynicism or despair?

Here the reply comes in two parts, the second of which is surprising. The first part of an answer is as follows: 'That which is, already has been; that which is to be, already has been' (3.15a). This effectively repeats what we already know, that excessive effort, the fantasy of control, over and above proper participation and enjoyment, is simply going against the grain of time. We have already been taught that going with the rhythms of life is a matter of great delicacy, involving experience, sense and faith in God's goodness.

But the second part of the answer is this: 'God seeks what has been driven away' (3.15b). The nature of the future in God is that the past may be redeemed. The errors we commit, the opportunities (or times) missed or violated, cannot be controlled or recovered by us. Indeed, our attempts to control time are how we miss or corrupt opportunities. But implied in this account of providence at work in and through time is the notion of the redemption of time.

So in the very last phrase of the verses we have read we have an anticipation of the recovery of time in Jesus Christ. For us, as Christians, God's work in time is brought to perfection in Christ. The Preacher offers an account of time not only as succession or sequence, but also as event, as constructed by appropriate events and, as such, also containing what we might call debris. Implied in this account, there is also a recovery of time, when God's blessing revealed in the gift of time will be brought to completion. And we believe Christ to be the centre of time: the point in time through which all of creation is brought to the fullness of God's love and purpose, and time is redeemed.

13

Religion in English everyday life

In presenting a book one has written,[1] one is confronted with the task of deciding what it is one has said. This is not necessarily very easy, given that the book took a long time to write and that throughout the writing I was beset by other duties. Much of the interest now is to hear what other people (other scholars, from other disciplines) make of it; indeed, in part what I have to say is in response to certain critics and reviewers. I am going to touch on four topics: first, religion; then method; next, discrimination or distinction; and lastly, religion again.

Religion

Perhaps the best way of opening up the discussion is to say that the book arises out of a certain experience, one that is both anthropological and priestly. For the core of the book – sixty thousand out of a hundred thousand words – is a study of the parish of Kingswood, where, between 1985 and 1988, I served my curacy. There is also a shorter piece, about the life of the church in the Cambridgeshire village of Comberton, where I lived during my training for the priesthood at theological college. These two parts contain ethnography; they attempt to describe everyday life in those places and the values that organize it; and – according to my mother – these are the interesting parts of the book.

But I have placed them within a framework of discussion, a discussion of some of the implications of these studies concerning the kind of social science that is productive – how, on this basis, one might fruitfully consider religion and study it, and what the place of religion is in everyday life: how it contributes, what its forms of existence and continuity are. So, without interfering in the descriptions too much, I attempt both to offer a contribution to the related academic disciplines (often fighting demons and spirits that are imperceptible to those outside the fraternity), and at the same time, to say something about certain pastoral and political questions that are of very wide interest in our society, not least to believers, and which focus around the notion of secularization, and the future of religion.

However, it must be emphasized that when I undertook the ethnographic descriptions, these wider matters were not my concern, except negatively: I found 'religion' as such not a very useful concept, and I wished to give a description of how people lived, first in a village, then in the Bristol suburb where I was placed, without recourse to it. The word 'religion' does not appear in either of the ethnographic parts, and I make no appeal to the Sociology of Religion literature in either study. I have a background as a social anthropologist: I was trained at the Oxford Institute of Social Anthropology, and I have done extensive fieldwork in France – in Paris, Toulouse and the foothills of the Pyrenees. That is enough on religion, the first time round, for it had no place in my original concerns. Let us turn now to questions of method.

Method

I have discovered that reviews come in two classes: the pompous and the not pompous – ones where the writer says 'This is not the book I would have written', and ones which try to discern the author's intentions. Both kinds, however, have raised questions as to method, on the one hand asking, what difference does it make that the writer is a priest?, and, on the other, what actually were the methods employed, for the author is very discreet? How was the research done?

From my remarks so far, it will be clear that the book is anthropological, not theological, and nor is it an account of being a priest in a place. Nevertheless, while I was doing my curacy, I was greatly helped by my fieldwork experience and this in two respects: both in the techniques learnt of paying attention, and in the sense of not expecting to be needed. Anthropological experience and the business of Christian ministry correspond quite well in certain regards. For as an anthropologist, one's job is not to make all the difference, but to learn to see differences at work. And likewise a priest is required to pay attention, to learn discernment. The other side of that is seeing that you yourself are not necessary to the situation: a clue to discernment is self-effacement. In fieldwork, that is obvious, for the problem is rather to learn to discern what effects are due to one's presence, and to discount them; it is not one's task gloriously to cause endless alteration. But the same is true, in a less obvious way, for the priest, in ways that could be elucidated. As an anthropologist, I was well reconciled to having no useful task in a place, to being neither needed nor, necessarily, liked, and to spending my time instead watching, paying attention and, in particular, noticing when I was not getting things right, when I was not understanding: in short, watching out for anomalies.

The business of spotting anomalies brings us closer to responding to the second aspect concerning method: the (sometimes irritably expressed) question, what do anthropologists do in the field? The answer is, they look for anomalies, that is, a non-match between expectation and event. There are a number of clues, in the footnotes and in the text, as to the mechanics of this kind of research, and they are fairly obvious. In the Kingswood monograph, for example, there are references to archive work, to local library collections and local government documents, to over sixty family histories, and to court reports in local newspapers. There are also a good many references to contemporary sociological accounts of similar places, almost constituting a history of local studies.[2] But all these sources are in a sense secondary, in that they provide materials for the employment of a certain sort of 'anthropological intelligence'. I have published an article on the conditions for exercising such intelligence.[3] Here, the question comes down to, how does learning detachment in the anthropological sense match up with exercising a Christian ministry? I have two things to say.

First, I have perhaps put things rather bleakly, but in practice, after an initial period, my experience in the parish was anything but bleak. One of the principal experiences I worked upon to write the ethnography was my sense of pleasure simply at being in the place – a quite involuntary intensity, not unlike falling in love, which I first felt and realized while standing in a queue in a bread shop, but was also manifested by the sense of well-being and physical relaxation that I experienced as I travelled on the long bus journey back to the parish after being away from Bristol on business in London. This is understanding born out of desire.[4]

And second, it is also true that, in practice, I undertook the anthropological study in order to perform my job better, in particular, to take funerals. For it very quickly became clear to me that I did not read at sight the criteria by which people judged lives well- or ill-lived, or intuitively understood the values that organized their lives together. The case that started me off was when I went to a house to discuss the funeral of a woman in her late eighties. Her daughter, a sensible, practical woman in her sixties, a grandmother herself, said to me in all sincerity, 'I really do not know what I shall do now mother has died'. This sense of loss was far more acute than I would have expected, for whether or not one misses one's mother of eighty-plus, for a person like me, it cannot easily be construed as being the loss of a world. Yet for this woman – and this was not a pathological case – her elderly mother was the linchpin of how her world was organized: a centre to the rhythms of daily life, the key to the patterns of family life, visiting and support, and through them, to how one lived – for over sixty years – in a particular small locality. This one remark opened up for me all kinds of understanding in due course, and also, I think, helped me to conduct the occasional offices with an increasing grasp of local realities. And once you can understand some of the resulting patterns, families are physically laid out before you at these services, in church, at a wedding, for example, where territory is to a degree reproduced in seating; quarrels (and movings away) are mirrored in gaps between bodies, and an endless calculus of differences, expressed, lived out, negotiated, is displayed.

It is perhaps worth adding that such an approach is a help from a purely personal point of view, for it gives two reasons for doing every job, which is a recipe for being content: every visit, every encounter contributes to your understanding, enabling you to confirm and develop what you have learnt, or else to modify and correct it. You put yourself at the service of the job with a whole heart.

To develop the argument a little more, it is clear that there is a duty of discretion. Or to put it more clearly, one's interest in understanding must always be at the service of one's pastoral task, and not vice versa. But I have come to the conclusion that this is no disadvantage for, effectively, human knowledge is always properly at the service of the people whom one is with – and the exploitative use of academic knowledge bears real parallels with forms of bad behaviour in real life. This brings us to my third point, concerning 'distinction' or discrimination.

Discrimination

In other words, the approach I have outlined – a social-anthropological discipline of paying attention – only mimics what is more generally the case: people make sense of life as well as live it, and they do both better or worse. Now, in the parish, the forms of life that are better or worse can be categorized, as 'respectable' on the one hand, and 'feckless' on the other. And I have mapped out to a detailed extent the workings of these complex collective categories: how people classify themselves and others in sets of claims to recognition – to distinction, or personality – and the weighings of these claims. I must emphasize that, in these claims and evaluations, nobody would ever suppose themselves to be feckless; all lie on the right side of the divide, in their own estimation; but this does not mean the opposition is not a powerful tool for effecting discriminations. I have also outlined in some detail how membership of certain public institutions, such as churches or chapels, can constitute a way both of sustaining these claims to personality, and of evaluating them, and how membership, too, is negotiated in a series of more or less intense forms of participation. So, if one wants to understand how churches and chapels are used in everyday life, it is necessary to pay attention to these questions of what might be called the 'division of symbolic labour', or how people participate differently in the field of evaluation created around these institutions. And I suggest ways that these dynamics of claim and evaluation operate more broadly, in different parts of local society, not simply including some and excluding others, but generating different, startlingly different, sorts of behaviour, and unexpected consequences.

Reverting to the question of method, it is worth remarking that this business of discrimination, of claiming distinction and evaluating that claim, or of how people make sense of and in their situation, is the key to an anthropological approach. It means giving the actors some kind of priority, and has numerous consequences in terms of what constitutes a social fact, and what understanding is, and how to appraise different kinds of social-scientific approach, and how to understand time. Indeed, the issue at stake could be said to be comprehending the social nature of time. For the whole book in a sense is about time: about how human experience can only be properly understood as constituted through apprenticeships, and therefore through time. And a major part of the personal interest of the project in its later stages has been learning techniques of writing that are compatible with and serve to express this temporal nature of human understanding, so that knowledge is not laid out in a single, simultaneous moment, open to an omnipotent gaze, but is sequential, relating to the gaining of insights (in the sense of being to do with the penny dropping), and never totalized. This concern again has implications as to what kinds of social science and modes of academic knowledge I am drawn to, and which sorts I reject. (The main chapters are silently structured around rejection or modification of accounts based upon gender, class and 'colonial theory'.)

I do not wish to elaborate the implications of this business of discrimination further now, except briefly to draw out a couple of consequences. The first is to re-emphasize that there are parallels between doing social anthropology and being a human being (a social *anthropos*). In the local landscape, there are persons of great respectability who participate in many aspects of public life: they not only embody certain values, but feel themselves able to represent these values publicly. They stand at one extreme. And there are also people who are less respectable: they are public personae, but in a different fashion – drinkers, fighters, womanizers. They in fact embody many of the same values: a sense of honour, of independence, of solidarity and generosity, but they cannot be held to embody public flourishing in the way the first class do. Now, just as there are good and less good forms of being human (in local terms), so there are good and less good forms of social science: science that respects human beings – in the sense of representing the values of human flourishing – and science that does not. Part of the fun of the bits of the book which my mother appreciated less is the delineation of what one might call a 'feckless' sociology, and its rationale. This sort of tendency is widespread among academics, especially in the social sciences; it might be characterized as relating to private honour but not to public good; and it is worth identifying it as bad human practice (or less than the best): poor scholarship, and poor behaviour.

Religion again

The other topic concerns the re-emergence of religion. This then is my last point. I set about my descriptions in terms that did not look to 'religion' as a useful category, and I have ended up with a consideration of how human beings live better or worse – and the place of such institutions as churches and chapels in these attempts. My suggestion now is that religion is how humans collectively pay attention to the conditions of human flourishing (and dysfunction), how they in practice meditate upon how to be fully human. Questions such as why fewer people come to church regularly, or attend chapel, than did so fifty years ago are then linked to questions about why fewer people feel themselves able publicly to sustain a claim to represent forms of human wellbeing than did so formerly. I shall not go further, except – since these are questions that move many people – to add three points, as it were, telegraphically.[5]

First, statistics – like share prices – go up and down, and the causes of their movements are not inherent to them: they do not contain the principle of their own explanation, in some occult fashion. Second, 'secularization' in this perspective is simply an increase in 'private' behaviour, or – to put it more positively – fewer people feel themselves bound up with an expression of a public good. This is a serious matter, but one with much wider social implications than those simply concerning church people, or religious sociologists. And third, neither 'pole' in the equation, which I have labelled 'respectability' and 'fecklessness' (or a self-identification with either 'public good' or 'private honour'), deriving these terms from a particular ethnography, is independent of the other: each position contains the full potential for its opposite to be realized. I call this the coinherence of opposites. And this is important for, even were the representatives of private honour to come to predominate for a while owing to a concatenation of conditions in Kingswood, they would contain within themselves the potential to regenerate respectability, the public forms necessary to a common life and well-being. So 'religion' not only re-emerges in the book as a topic, having been safely put out of the way; it emerges in the form of being glimpsed either in its partial realization, or in its absence.

I think these three points – which demand enormous elaboration – are interesting because they point to a way in which a certain kind of social science may contribute to theological debate, and even help to change some of its terms, while retaining its specificity and force. I should add that different forms of social science will appeal to different forms of theological mind, and just as there is 'privatized' social science, there may well be feckless theology.

The fate of the anthropologist

These conclusions all may follow from, as a cynical friend from theological college expressed it, my having been 'ordained anthropologist to serve in the parish of Kingswood' – from my partial identification of the tasks of anthropologist and Anglican priest. One of my teachers, Julian Pitt-Rivers, drily remarked to me that two American anthropologists who had conducted a small-town study featured in effigy in the town carnival the year after the publication of their book, portrayed as two apes shovelling dung. I trust my fate, in the long term, will be kinder.

14

Anglicanism: the only answer to modernity

In order to understand any institution, one needs to grasp the question to which it is a response. By doing so, one can offer a description of its essential components, including its characteristic virtues, modes of working and scale of operation. At the same time, one can avoid the anecdotal analysis of accidental features as if they were symptomatic. My aim is to offer an account of the Anglican vocation in this spirit. This account comes in three parts: the first concerning the setting to which it is a response; the second placing it within the broad context of Christian responses to this setting; and the third considering the specificity of the Anglican solution. My claim is that there is sufficient continuity in the situation for there to be enduring sense in the response.

The problem of modernity

To begin with, I want to characterize in broad terms the experience of being a Christian believer at this present time. This experience refers less to matters of belief or worship than to the interaction of faith with its context. In other words, I wish to ask to what extent the world seems to confirm or, on the contrary, threatens to deny that faith.

The experience to which I refer operates at three levels. First, at the smallest scale, referring to specific day-by-day experience – parish ministry, for example, or life at the local level in a particular locality – it appears by and large that – from the perspective of a believer – things are going quite well. Aspects of life make sense, the local church makes a difference, individuals come to faith, people try to live decent lives, and so forth. All believers go on trying to make sense of living faithfully, they have a ministry or a vocation among other things, and there appear to be enough materials in the surrounding world that help them do so. There appears to be a sufficient density of believers for the practices to sustain themselves – even when at quite low levels. That is, there is a worthwhile local engagement, expressed in worship, the development of a common life, and outreach or mission. (This is a useful characterization of the levels of Church life, to which we will return.)

And from within a wider Christian perspective, beyond the confines of the local church, there are always signs of life or forms of intensity of faith, such as lively churches, movements among the young, experiments with worship, and Pentecostalism.

At a second, broader level, however, there is quite a lot of disquiet. The world appears to be full of forces that are indifferent to faith. Whether it is the workings of money, or science's impersonal and relentless questioning, or technology's blind progress, in every case, people feel threatened. This threat is not simply physical, that, say of ecological disaster, or of eventual war, but because these forces also appear to undermine and diminish the values of human life and faith. This is so to such an extent that it may be fair to suggest that impersonal forces, in the form of greed and apathy, self-centredness and lack of discrimination, risk overturning the life of faith. In other words, the believer has a sense that, despite the experience that faith works and provides evidence to the Christian at the small scale of everyday life, on a wider scale there is a potential that the world will undermine or deny the possibility of that faith. There is an unfocused anxiety about what we might call the plausibility of faith, even for believers (or especially for believers).

This anxiety is expressed in the everyday in the way that a great many people, rather than living with any sense of crisis, appear to be able to live without recourse to faith. For these, apathy would be the best description, rather than hostility. And this sense can be expressed within the life of churches, in terms of low levels of commitment and in confusion of aims, in the sapping of energy and morale.

At a third, rather vast and unfocused level, there seems to be, against the second view, a belief in the ultimate goodness of the universe. People by and large believe, and Christians most earnestly believe, that God made the universe, and it is good, and it is for us: we are made for salvation, one might say, and salvation is a real possibility. Why people who appear indifferent to the specific claims of the Christian faith nevertheless seem to hold to the benignity of the cosmos quite as much as do believers might be held to constitute a puzzle. At the moment, however, I am simply concerned to note how widely the broad view is held, including by people who appear to be quite tough-minded.

Now people in the churches, both leaders and ordinary members, tend to play in and out of these three levels: personal experiences of order and glimpses of worth at a local level; a sense of impersonal forces and the threat of real destruction on a wider level; and a broad belief in providence, and the ultimate coming-right of things. The elements can be put together in different ways and played off against each other. You can underplay providence, in a pessimistic fashion, and suggest that the dark forces will probably overwhelm us, or you can suppose optimistically that we shall overcome the risks that beset us. We tend to use our perception and evaluation to back up our advocating a particular course of action.

To sum up, this view of the world has within it a curious sense of potential, both for good and for evil. There is a great uneasiness in it, a tension, that is increased by the double sense that here we have the elements of something very good, but at the same time, the possibility of making the most unutterable mess. We have a sense of the possibility of salvation, but we also fear damnation.

The birth of the modern world

What I want to ask, as the next step, is where this complex view of the world comes from. It is an interesting story. It is, roughly speaking, the history of the modern world, and it contains an account of what the Anglican Church is for.

To put matters crudely, the modern world was born in the sixteenth and seventeenth centuries when the Western Church fell into warring parts. It did so through the notion of freedom, and the right to follow one's own conscience. In the longer perspective, the principal question for human beings has not concerned freedom but how to promote their own flourishing and well-being, and the key to that has been the task of creating order, essentially a just order. Clearly, one needs elements of freedom, to impose sufficient order that people flourish, but freedom has never been the principal issue. The basic problem has always been not enough order, or the powerful abusing their freedom to exploit the rest. And the great achievement of medieval Christian Europe was to create a settlement in which order, freedom and human flourishing all served each other, at least to a degree.[1] This we call the feudal order, a divine settlement in which justice, power and production work together.

This order fell apart as the Church tried to promote its own interests against those of certain political powers. It insisted upon the right of resistance of believers to secular rulers who opposed its order.[2] In so doing, it created a monster, because the right of resistance was then invoked against the Church, in an outbreak of liberty or freedom taken as a sign of God's Spirit in the world. A period of extraordinary conflict followed. In brief, by promoting its own interests, the Church neglected to promote human flourishing: this is the trauma that lies at the origin of the modern world.

The trio of elements I have described became set against one another: order, in its (Roman) Catholic form, stood against freedom, in its

Reformed, Presbyterian embodiment, and human flourishing suffered mightily. Of course, order has plenty of freedom within it, just as freedom has in practice (possibly too much) order, and each party claimed that unopposed it was the way to human flourishing, but in practice, order and freedom – or superstition and enthusiasm, as Hume has it[3] – horribly blocked each other.

After three generations of religious wars, when, as Montaigne remarks, people acted more cruelly towards one another than had ever been the case in antiquity or among savages,[4] various leaders decided that peace, human flourishing, was a more pressing and more important demand than religious truth. In France, these leaders were called *les politiques*.[5] People in Western Europe had to take upon themselves the question of how to promote human flourishing, and they did so very seriously and, one might say, pragmatically. The moves to political science, and to economics, and to how to harness the natural world (and politics, economics and nature were all invented in their modern forms at this time), were undertaken in the knowledge that you cannot simply turn back to the Church and expect it to know best concerning human well-being. One might wish to, but one cannot: that is part of the modern experience.

Here we have some of the main elements of the experience of modernity that I have outlined: various sciences as ways of pursuing well-being, humans come of age, a certain pragmatism (see what will work, rather than being guided by tradition or by 'ultimate questions'), and the failure of religion. All these factors need to be taken seriously.

But there is another element needed to complete the picture. For, of course, just because religion cannot be relied upon does not mean you can turn your back on God. If pragmatism becomes your final horizon, human practices become idolatrous: politics becomes the pursuit of power, economics the seeking of wealth, science the domination of nature – and unintended consequences accumulate in an ever-accelerating fashion. That is no way to promote human flourishing – which was, if you remember, the point of the exercise. And here we have the sense of science, technology, the market and so forth as a threat – a threat both to our bodies and our souls.

Anglicanism as an answer

Anglicanism was actually born to meet this situation, and shares the same 'political' spirit. It is first of all a consecration of the political settlement that says order and freedom must both be present, but subordinate to human flourishing. Indeed, Anglicanism contains representative 'parties' favouring order, freedom and human well-being respectively. But the

settlement insists that their holding together in a common human project is more important than their independent – and sometimes incompatible – claims to truth.

Second, it is a consecration of the coming of age of the human: it at
once supports the world of modernity that was founded, and the human
ideal or vocation that underwrites it. And, at the same time, it has the
role of recalling these humans to the worship of the one true God, without which all pragmatism becomes idolatry. This is the point of 'establishment' in the English Church. It is a functional way of continually
drawing attention to the need on the part of all responsible people to
contest idolatry. What matters is less the form it takes, and more how
best to pursue the task.

Anglicanism, in sum, is a facing up of the Christian faith to the failure of religion, and the consequences of taking seriously the continuing project of creating human flourishing under these circumstances. I
am only half-joking when I say that Anglicanism is the only answer to
modernity.

Christian responses

Given this account of Anglicanism being well adapted to modernity, what
of the other churches? For Anglicanism is clearly only one settlement
among several, and somewhat atypical in the European context. To put
matters positively, what life do Christians have in common? What is
it that joins them together, beyond the fact that they go to various
churches, and therefore might be thought of as species of the genus
'churchgoer'? Do they share any real common life?

The answer to this question includes a historical dimension, as we
have seen. In Europe – and beyond – we are indelibly marked by
the Reformation, and how the Reformation and its consequences are
understood shapes whether one sees any common life to Christians. The
commonest position is one that prolongs the contemporary perceptions
of that period and which divides the actors in the Reformation into
good men and villains: good Christians and not-really Christians.
You may call the latter misguided, or foolish, or wicked, or even anti-
Christians, but there is no doubt that there is a distribution of being
right and being wrong. It is quite hard, under these circumstances, to
envisage any practical common life to Christians in the present. A
common life is envisaged in the past, before the Fall/Reformation, or
in the future, after repentance for past folly or, most likely, at the
Eschaton, but there is never any common life today.

It is possible, however, to offer another view of the Reformation, one
that does not divide Christians into the good and the bad. Rather, the

Reformation is the fragmentation of the Western Catholic Church, and the fragments are all true parts of the Body of Christ. Each and every expression of the Christian faith is the work of God in believers: evidence of the ongoing action of Christ for us.

Two things need to be said, one quite complicated, the other quite simple. The complicated thing is this. Just because God is to be found in every church, this does not mean that every church is equivalent. From what has been said before, the difference may be put as follows: each church is a balance of the three elements of order, freedom and human flourishing. They correspond in part to tradition, revelation and reason. The question is, to which do you give priority? The older churches tend to privilege order as the key to freedom in Christ and to consequent human flourishing. The newer churches tend to privilege freedom (of conscience) as the key to order and to consequent human flourishing. The Anglican Church, because it was born in the struggle between the advocates of order and those of freedom, tends to suggest that order and freedom should be subservient to human flourishing; in other words, keep your eye on the end, and use the appropriate means. This in fact gives quite another view about how to behave in the world, and what is an appropriate scale for action, and indeed, knowledge. More 'principled' Christian churches tend to regard this pragmatism with suspicion, and sometimes disdain.

But the overall point is that all churches have these three serious theological elements – order, freedom and human flourishing – in play, and they constantly debate their relation, whether in respect to common life, worship or mission. And how they balance them determines many differences. The differences are important, but should be recognized for what they are, differences in balance rather than differences in essence.

This brings us to the second, simple point, which is crucial. If we believe that faith is not owned by the believer, not produced by him or her, but rather is the evidence of God's activity in us, then the faith to be found in every believer, and therefore in every church, is put into them by God. In which case, to neglect or disparage the faith of others is literally blasphemous: turning our backs upon God's embodied action. In practice, this is a hard saying. But this critique is implied by the Anglican settlement, which sees the world as the sphere of God's action, and therefore the faith of others as truly faithful, though not identical to the Anglican vocation. One should not, of course, expect symmetry of recognition between the different Christian settlements in such a perspective, nor does it obtain.

The situation of the Christian churches

That being so, Anglicanism's vocation is set within this pluralist context; it is one viable response to the modern situation. It is of course a difficult situation, in that it is complex. It is neither a Godless world, nor one that is clearly religious. More complicated still, the secular world that has been created itself oscillates between demanding order and seeking freedom, each taken on its own as a complete answer to the problem of human well-being. Advocates of authority, order and science, for example, engage in a dialogue of the deaf with promoters of the free market and a morality of individualism. The debates between these total answers generate much of what causes us doubt and even fear. Certainly, they obscure the calling to promote Godliness and human flourishing by subordinating both order and liberty to these projects. So it is often difficult to articulate the Christian calling in its specificity, and in general it is something that we do better than talk about, for good reason, as pursuing human flourishing and the worship of God are essentially practices, not theories. But let me try and articulate that calling a little.

From the point of view of Christian people, our vocation will have a number of forces or constraints at work giving it shape. We are called to be Christians, to follow Christ. That call does not go away. Yet, because we are all adult and competent, the Church community is divided in its perception of what is important and what its aims are.

Religion is widely distrusted, and its public image in this respect is very different to the believer's experience of it. There are few points of contact between people's personal involvement with and commitments to the Christian faith and the public accounts of religion. And yet, on the negative side, there are sufficient examples of abuses of power, acts of idiocy and wickedness attributable to religious people to make it difficult to build a strong public case for the Church.

The demand for flourishing, or salvation, is however widely felt, and pursued by other means, often through institutions that the Church shares in the provision of, relating to schooling, hospitals, care, welfare and charities. We might note that thinking about these institutions is never finished, never perfected, and that the Church may have future as well as past roles to play in these activities. And this is for the following reason: the ever-present threat of idolatry, or the collapse of horizons from the ideal to the pragmatic, and even the self-interested. For the life of institutions continually threatens the projects they carry; this is true of every institution, whether it is the Church, the health service, transport, education of the young, care of the elderly, trade, the provision of food or of energy. In short, modernity has not resolved the problem of sin.

The Anglican vision

If this description is in any sense valid, how might we set about articulating the Anglican vision – saying who we are, and why we are,
offering a way of articulating a way of living? Note that this articulation has to be done in a certain kind of way. We cannot, for example,
simply offer a set of first-order principles to define how we should
behave, for this is one of the ways of making sense that has been dis-
credited in the fall of religion. Likewise, we cannot claim that the
individual lives in a world where he (or she) is free to make sense as
best he can. The emphasis upon the priority of human flourishing, and
the recourse both to order and to freedom as appropriate to serve that
aim, has implications for how one proceeds intellectually, implications –
as we shall see – both as to scale and style of engagement.

This account will consider Anglicanism simply within its English
context. It is worth remarking that in developing an account of the
Anglican vocation, we are led necessarily to narrow the scope to an intermediate scale, situated between global claims and individual needs. This
is because of the sort of settlement with which we are concerned.
Nevertheless, it is not by that a parochial vision. One of the surprising
features of attending international Anglican gatherings is that there are
churches represented from countries outside the sphere of former
British rule or influence, Japan, Rwanda, the Congo and Brazil among
them. One reason for the transferrable nature of this form of Christianity to places that are or have been troubled in different ways lies, I
suggest, in the form of the settlement that Anglicanism represents, a
settlement that, if not capable of resolving the antinomies of the
modern condition, is at least capable of holding them in tension.

I shall approach the task through a set of four questions and answers.
First, what does the Church offer this country? Then, what is the basis
of the Church's uniqueness? Following that, what is the specificity of
the Anglican Church? And finally, what then is the role of the Anglican
Church? We need not be confined to these four questions, and they are
of course extremely general. But they lend us a certain orientation and
take us a certain way, giving rise to a number of matters that could be
pursued in more detail.

The first question, then, is what the Church offers this country. We
are concerned at this stage with the whole Christian Church. The answer
might be, in a suitably Trinitarian formula, three things: first, charity, or
the givenness of God; second, the forgiveness of sins, or the way of God
in Christ; and third, hope, or the work of the Spirit. Each of these characteristics is clearly capable of extraordinary elaboration, but that is not
my point here, which is rather to consider what signs or resources the

Church bears for the society of which it is a part. Each of these characteristics, indeed, is borrowed by other, secular institutions, or simulated by them; even 'saying sorry' has had its moment. However, the claim that limitless generosity and true forgiveness and real hope – rather than, say, calculation, repression and illusion – are the basis of intelligibility and being in this world is the mark of the Christian Church.

The Church bears witness to the possibility, and more, the reality, of generosity, forgiveness and hope, and that is what the Church is good for, in the eyes of the rest of the social order. Of course, the possibility of charity, redemption and hope are frequently denied in secular discourse, and equally frequently, the Church's adequacy to the task of conveying such possibilities is (often rightly) contested. Nevertheless, if you want to understand the sort of resources the Church offers the country, its particular function or uniqueness, these are the sort of questions to which you will have to look.

So the second question is, what is the basis, in practice, of the Church's uniqueness? Here the answer is worship. Worship defines the specificity of the Church's contribution, which might be termed as being ministry in, to and against the society it serves. The Church is organized above all else to provide regular, well-ordered, lively worship, for worship is the lifeblood of the Church.

It is true that the Church should offer a model of community, and that it should pay attention to acts of charity, and that it should join in public reflection upon the way society should go. This is not a plea for the narrowing of the Church's vision and task. But it is to claim that all affirmation, questioning and criticism of the social order is initially perceived and articulated when a common life is offered up, reflected upon and judged through worship and the reading of Scripture in worship. Other sources of affirmation, questioning and criticism need to be taken up and used, but they need to be subjected to criteria that emerge from the business of worship.

Otherwise, the Church simply takes up other discourses, essentially humanistic, pragmatic discourses with their inevitable tendency to idolatry. I have suggested that these discourses tend to take their lowered horizon of expectation, which is to pursue human well-being in a particular context, as an ultimate horizon, and thereby they come to defeat their own purpose. To adopt such an approach is doubly a defeat for the Church, for its task in joining in public discussions is to point to the demands and possibility of God, while at the same time affirming the goodness of the project of promoting the public good, and without making monopolistic (and foolish) claims for the place and importance of the Church. And the Church can only achieve this complex task through regular worship. I will return to this in the last section.

It may be that the millennial task of the Church of England is to make sure that collective daily prayer is going on in all its churches (not Bible studies and quiet times, but regular public worship), and that that will be enough for it to fulfil its calling. It is within its compass to achieve; it has the resources and the buildings. Nobody could object that the Church was straying into territory that is not its own. And the steady supply of (one hopes) increasing numbers of people daily confronted by Scripture and its demands, and ordering their lives around its demands in prayer, would leaven public life in quite unforeseeable ways. So, to repeat, the Church's uniqueness is based upon worship.

The third question that follows is, then, what is the specificity of the Anglican Church? For all that I have said so far applies to all the Christian Churches. As I have already suggested, each Church is defined out of its history by a particular relation to state and people, an ideal model of self-definition and authority, which we might term a political settlement. The Anglican relation to the polity is lived out in two particular and related forms, which respond to the various demands of scale, inclusiveness, human autonomy and style which I have sketched. These two forms may be labelled as 'territorial embeddedness' (which occurs at several levels: parish, diocese and nation) and a 'conversational mode'.

These two forms in fact constrain the aspects of Anglican ordained ministry. On the one hand, a priest takes on a territory and all the peo-ple in it, without exception, as his or her responsibility: the cure of souls. This aspect corresponds to the doctrine of the Incarnation: it is the case that God is to be found embodied in a particular place, locality, people; the materials of time and history can show him forth. (Which is why any ministry is an experiment in providence, finding out how God is present in a place.) And on the other hand, he or she has to engage conversationally, rather than authoritatively, or in an exclusive fashion. This is because no one voice, opinion or understanding can hold an ex-haustive account of the glory of God, and only through conversation are our blindnesses remedied. This aspect corresponds to the doctrine of the mystery of God.

You might remark two negative features of Anglican ministry, or what are often taken to be so: the Anglican Church does not gather like-minded people, nor does it claim a monopoly on the truth. But these characteristics emerge from a positive theology: an understanding of God's working in history as an expression of his character, and a response to it.

We might notice two more things here. These two features – terri-torial embeddedness and a conversational mode – serve to identify the two characteristic forms of the ministry of the Anglican Church: the gathering of a congregation drawn from a particular place, and what I think of as 'chaplaincy' – being out and about, taking an interest, and 'being used to think with' (in shorthand). This needs to be explored, but it is worth remarking here that much of the Anglican Church's work, at every level (up to the national), is performed in this chaplaincy style: for example, in the bishop's public role in the diocese as much as the priest's around the parish. Note, too, that in a society where, for the moment, fewer people feel licensed or committed or compelled to come to church, 'chaplaincy' will continue to be enormously important to fulfilling the Church's calling. But it must also be said that this work cannot be done without worshipping congregations underwriting it. Both forms are vital, and depend upon each other.

The second thing to note is that such an understanding of the specificity of the Anglican Church (in terms of territory and conversation, congregation and chaplaincy) has a considerable flexibility built into its relations at different levels with a developing polity. One important feature is that the Anglican Church need not be understood as tied through establishment to a particular notion of the nation-state, nor need each parish church or diocesan cathedral be seen as a function of that model of polity.

The fourth (and last) question is, what then is the role or vision for the Anglican Church? Since the Church is embedded and conversational, I cannot tell you in satisfying detail; it has to be worked out on site. But let me say this. The basic issue has not changed since the time of the Venerable Bede (who recorded the Christianization of Britain): the Church has a crucial role to play in the creation and maintenance of a just and peaceful society, so that people may live ordered, quiet and faithful lives. Its concern is human flourishing, which we call salvation, or the kingdom of God. I acknowledge that one needs to be cautious in making such claims, and that sensible people immediately want to emphasize the eschatological element; that is, to say that the kingdom of God is not simply human well-being. But I want to make two points by putting things as I do. First, there is a point in concentrating upon human particularities, and not reaching too quickly for the eschatological. Christians need to think against an eschatological horizon, but in a grounded way that might lend some content to the concept. And second, salvation is what the human heart truly desires, and so, the other way about, such things as the human heart truly desires – such as health, and peace, and company, and dying well – have to be comprehended in an account of salvation. Otherwise, once again, we have no content to the concept: it simply trumps human concerns. All that being said, because the issues have not changed, the basic tasks of the Church are the same, even though one must pay attention to the various scales upon which human lives are constructed, and to the constraints created by the recent history described.

In brief, the tasks of the Church are worship, exemplarity or witness, education and call. The congregation's calling is to live and worship locally, welcoming the alien, helping the poor and oppressed, expressing a life in common with other congregations in the place, trying to live out the reality of charity, forgiveness and hope. To this should be added the business of education, both of selves and others, whereby both the principles and practices of flourishing should be explored and transmitted; and the call made to all classes, professions, trades and persons to live up to the height of their calling. All these tasks emphasize the tension between everyday life and the life of the congregation that structures the Anglican vocation.

Intensification and extensity

As a last step, I want to develop a little on two of the topics that have emerged, once again narrowing the scale. Earlier, I suggested that the life of any church, no matter how small, is focused at three levels – in worship, the development of a common life, and outreach. I want to look in particular at the first and the last: the intensification of worship and the extension of reach, of interest and connection (which is sometimes called mission). These are mediated, of course, by the life of the worshipping community. But if we say that the business of the church is worship, common life and outreach, and if we know that the life in all these is the life of God's spirit and not the force of our own wills, then the intensification of worship must be the key to any attempt at development.

The resource for any intensification of faith in our tradition is prayer and reading the Bible, but prayer and reading the Bible have to be put in the context of liturgical worship. This is a complex area; let me try and put things briefly.[6]

First, churches should aim to conduct daily prayer, in a structured form. This is within the compass of most congregations; it demands a small group that feels the call to sustain such a project.

Second, the point of using a liturgy is that it offers a transforming structure. The participants are altered as they pass through it, purged as it were of their own wills and desires, and opened to the mind of God. In this way, their prayers are curiously distanced from their desires, hopes and fears – though not indifferent to them.

Third, this transformation is achieved in large part, I am convinced, by the reading of Scripture in worship. The Bible is the face of God, and in worship, rather than reading the Bible, we are read by it. This business of being read is, again, not a simple matter. We are concerned on the one hand with the way that the Scriptures respond to and converse with one another, being re-read to apply to new situations – most notably, of course, but by no means uniquely, the appearance of the Messiah. And we are concerned on the other hand with reading our own situation analogously with the eyes of faith. This process – of being read by Scripture – is not simple application, but rather the discernment of an always-provisional logic of faith. We are very bad at it in the contemporary Church; it is a skill that we have to relearn.

Fourth, and finally, what then occurs in worship is that the participants bring in the world about, in their concerns, desires, fears and so forth. They are reordered by the complicated business of being read by Scripture in the course of the liturgy, and freed to pray. And these transformed creatures then go out to that world about: that world has been subtly changed, because it has been prayed for, and the participants are also subtly changed, a leaven to effect growth and so to continue this dialectic of worship and world.

All that is in shorthand. My claim is that the Bible read in worship is a means of intensification of faith. Using it so is an extraordinary challenge, because we scarcely know how to do it. But doing so is within our compass – we have the numbers, and the will, and the means. And, to repeat an earlier point, nobody would deny that that is what the Church is for, whether or not they approve the project.

From this outline, you can see why I believe extension of reach goes hand in hand with this intensification of faith. I will be briefer still on this topic. Learning about the setting of one's faith has to do with what one brings into prayer, but it also has to do with the division of labour. Some will concentrate upon the life of the congregation, and worship, and outreach. Others have principally to take an interest in the place as a whole, make an inventory of institutions, employments, interests and so forth – in short, map out the place in all its dimensions. For example, if you do not know your farmers and the state of the farming industry by the time foot and mouth hits, you have left it too late. Both kinds of activity – the congregational and chaplaincy – relate to the other. One gives a content to faith and worship; the other gives a point to knowing about the place. They are complementary forms of ministry; together, they form a matrix which may serve the people around, who share the calling to promote human flourishing, but need resources to do so.

In short, engagement with the world and worship of the Christian God cannot be detached from one another. Serious worship of God and being taken seriously by the world are complementary projects, and not opposed. This is our central challenge, and should shape all our thinking about ministry. It seems to me there is no other way of responding to our vocation, if I have perceived it aright: a vocation of affirming a world where man has come of age, where the demand to worship God is as real as it always has been, and where the consequences of idolatry are as clear as ever they have been.

15

Unfashionable virtues: forbearance

The virtues take us to the heart of how to live a Christian life. Virtues are not rules, or even ends in themselves, but dispositions or attitudes, habits of mind and behaviour that allow us to take part in a project. As such, they are as much collective properties as individual, for they are shared and inculcated by a collective way of life, by the Church. And it is only by taking the virtues on, and exploring them, and living them out, that one comes to join in that way of life and learn what it is about.

So virtues are concerned with living a way of life and, we might add, each way of life will have its own characteristic virtues that are internal to it. We are, of course, principally concerned with a Christian way of life. But it is worth adding that, from within a given way of life, other ways of life will appear quite odd, for one will not readily have the criteria to judge them by. Each way of life produces its own rules to live by, its own dispositions within which these rules make sense, and what we might call its own evidence – for each way of life produces its own goods or outcomes.

To take an extreme example of a way of life, taking certain drugs is a collective phenomenon, with its own codes and values, justifications and outcomes. It is usually exclusive of other ways of life, and it contains its own fate.

We might sum up this point of view by saying that who you become depends on the company you keep, and the gods they worship. This perspective is a constant in the Bible, in the Old Testament and the New: everything comes down, in an important sense, to the group of people you belong to and the practices they engage in.

The matter is explored in some detail in the book of Judges, for example, where the contrast is made between following the God of the Hebrews and following the gods of the Canaanites in the Promised Land. This, indeed, is the structuring opposition of the entire book. Each way of life has its own dispositions and produces its own confirmatory evidence. If you follow the God of the Hebrews, you explore the possibility that the world is ordered according to a principle of generosity, or blessing, and the appropriate forms of behaviour include attitudes of faith, and participation in that blessing, so that you yourself express that generosity. If however you follow the gods of the Canaanites, you explore the idea that the world is ordered by a principle of equivalence. Whereupon there are different appropriate forms of response, including calculation of the odds, a focus on self-interest, and what one might call a concept of limited good, so that one gets out what one puts in. These are very different ways of living in the world, and very different virtues are involved. What is more, each way of life produces its own confirmatory evidence. By and large, for perfectly good technical reasons, the way of faith is slower to deliver and less definable in its outcomes than the way of calculating self-interest. Nevertheless, according to the Bible, the way of faith is surer, and more enduring. That is the lesson of the promises of God, of the Exile, and of the coming of the Messiah.

So it is unsurprising that the Bible contains explorations, often in the form of lists, of the dispositions or virtues that enable the way of life to which the followers of God are called. These explorations are often incorporated in other sorts of discussions, though sometimes set apart, and occur in a variety of places. They are always involved in reflection on the character of the God who is known through his nature as generosity or blessing. Take, for example, the account from Isaiah of the Rod of Jesse, the chosen ruler in whom the requisite virtues exist that will play a crucial role in bringing in the kingdom of God, including the recovery of the lost of Israel and the recognition of the Gentiles. It is a compact passage, but the virtues outlined are the key to the fulfilment of God's purposes. And this list was adopted by the Church, and taken as the precursor to a characteristic set of Christian virtues.

Paul, of course, offers us his own lists, drawn up with precisely the same aim in mind. He wishes to give what are simultaneously the conditions for creating and participating in a community orientated around the God and Father of our Lord Jesus Christ. The lists drawn up later by the Christian Church take on Paul's insights, as well as drawing on the Old Testament. Essentially, their lists take the three chief virtues of faith, hope and charity, which can be construed to be expressions of the Hebrew God explored in the book of Judges and elsewhere, the defining forms of participation in the God of blessing. And they combine them with the four virtues described by pagan philosophers: the virtues of prudence, temperance, courage and justice (which would have been recognizable to Canaanite sages, interestingly enough).

Dispositions

The virtues as we have them, then, describe dispositions thought necessary to participate in a community that comes to something, the something being Christian ends. And we might note that the virtues are mixed, in the sense that some are revealed while others are constructed by reason.

Now, in one sense, all virtues are unfashionable, to the extent that there are always more obvious ways of life on offer, with more immediate goods to share in. That indeed was the problem of living in the Promised Land: Canaanite goods seemed a good deal more attractive than Hebrew goods, for they delivered their rewards – such as power, wealth and fertility – more speedily, to the extent that the Hebrew faith became diluted, distorted, fragmented and largely forgotten. Read the book of Judges. Were it not, indeed, for the faithfulness of God, it is quite clear that the faith – and its appropriate virtues – would have disappeared.

And this gives more focus to our topic, for this notion of virtue allows us to identify what is at issue in our trying to live a faithful life now, under contemporary conditions. What are the collective dispositions we need to cultivate and embody and encourage in one another in order to live Christian lives here and now, to reasonable Christian ends, in a viable Christian community? It has never been a simple or straight-forward task to live by faith in this world, and it certainly is not now; it is a continuing task to discern the values and ends to live by, not to mention the company one ought to keep.

Forbearance is clearly related both to temperance and to prudence. But its unfashionableness comes out when you consider its contraries – for example, impulsiveness and outspokenness. A certain spontaneity and frankness, we might call them, are often considered desirable character traits, even though we may think them overrated in extreme cases. And forbearance, the other way about, appears an ambiguous characteristic. On the one hand, it may be thought to be admirable to be patient, and not moved to premature or unnecessary expression of the self. But only up to a point, for on the other hand, such an attitude can seem to lend itself to self-effacement, and perhaps a lack of confidence in one's judgement, and even to contribute in this way to a person's vulnerability, to their being led astray, compromised, or even seduced. So the idea of forbearance raises the question of where is the centre of judgement that relates to other ways of life, which is simultaneously reserved and secure.

The issue lies in the fact that the virtues – these dispositions – are collective. You cannot be secure in your own judgement, as a rock, without reference to others. And yet, you cannot be absolutely confident in the bearings you gain from others in any given instant. There is no assured consensus; rightly or wrongly, we believe that is the mark of modern life: we live in the midst of a plurality of values. I am set in the midst of various projects and ways of life, and I am neither independent of them nor superior to them, so how am I to judge for myself and to live virtuously?

Austen's Persuasion

It is unsurprising that novels are a major resource for reflecting on this issue, for they usually offer a narrative constructed at the scale at which humans interact and make sense (or folly). And it is not an original observation that Jane Austen's novels offer a series of detailed considerations of how to live a virtuous life under modern conditions. Alasdair MacIntyre draws attention to the central place of constancy and amiability in Jane Austen's account of a virtuous life, and also to the importance of her Christian faith. I would suggest that each novel explores a particular virtue, and that the relevant one for us is her last novel, *Persuasion*, which places forbearance at the centre.

The heroine, Anne Elliot, is the member of three interconnected social circles (defined by house names), which simultaneously constitute her resources and her limits, for they each have their distinctive flaws. First, her own family has rank, property and good looks – all of which are, for Austen, desirable. And yet they are so conscious of these blessings that they are vain, and so limited in perception by that vanity that in the pursuit of their ideals and pleasures they consult neither their real interests nor their dignity.

Anne owes her common sense and discernment to her mother, now deceased, who – despite her good sense – had married an attractive and empty man for his looks. Anne sees the flaws of her family, though probably not in the round, but they do not repel her as they repel the reader. She is both at home and not at home, and forbearance is almost second nature to her. She does not utter the judgements she forms, even as she tries to promote the dignity of her father and elder sister, nor does she desire to break the ties and live a new life. She is, we might think, curiously passive; she is certainly neither outspoken nor impulsive.

These qualities serve her well in the second of her circles, that connected with her married younger sister, who has settled three miles away with her husband's family. Here again there are characteristic virtues and vices, good-heartedness and kindliness on the one hand, but little education or powers of discrimination on the other. The lack of these is rarely felt in the day-to-day, but can emerge in matters of unwise behaviour, lack of foresight and, on a single occasion, a dangerous – though avoidable – accident.

Anne is serviceable in this company, again because she does not say what she sees, but acts with constant kindness and with insight, to supplement what is lacking and to attempt to reconcile conflicts. Hers is a practical rather than an abstract intelligence. She tries to bring good out of the situation, often by prolonging matters, and easing them where possible. And she does not bring a superior mind to bear, offering judgement, but forbearing from comment, refraining from joining in or passing on criticism, and refusing to take sides. She tries to play her part, not to pass on the bad, and to promote the good.

As well as being modest in the scope of her ambition, her practical wisdom is also quite limited in what it seeks to achieve. She wishes at times that people might behave other than they do, but she does not think it likely. Her forbearance comes out not simply in her behaviour but in her accurate appraisal of her own powers and limits, both in her power to understand and in her power to cause things to happen.

The third circle consists in the household of a widowed friend of her mother's who, on the latter's account, had settled near Anne's family home. She is Anne's godmother, the only person to appreciate Anne's character or disposition, to value her discernment and taste, her quiet self-effacement, and her readiness to be of service. All the same, she too has both strengths and weaknesses; perhaps too high a regard for property, rank and a secure place in the world (although these are highly desirable goods), and perhaps too little insight into minds quicker than or different to her own.

These properties in fact make her a menace to Anne at two crucial points. One is when, before the story starts, she dissuaded the young Anne from marrying the estimable Captain Wentworth, on the perfectly reasonable grounds that he lacked fortune and she experience of the world. The other is when she tries to persuade Anne to marry the inscrutable John Elliot, nephew and heir to her father's estate, thinking that his character would match what she supposed she knew of his rank and fortune. That is to say, contrary to Anne's practice, she assumed both an insight she did not have and a power to discern and determine future events.

Anne's situation in broad terms is one with which we might consider ourselves to be familiar. She has no resources with which she is completely in harmony, or can rely on without reflection, and yet she is in solidarity with these social circles; effectively, they constitute who she is. She has certain supplementary powers – as we all have – for she can think, and judge, and act for herself, but she has no guarantees that she will think clearly, or judge well, or act to her own long-term advantage or well-being.

In these circumstances, forbearance is critical. Anne is decisive enough in moments of crisis, usually precipitated by the lack of circumspection of others, but she does not strike out on her own account. She waits, for it is clear that impulsiveness or outspokenness would usually lend strength to forms of folly, or would close down options for good.

Two things need to be added. First, it is clear forbearance cannot stand on its own, but needs other virtues to work with, perhaps especially constancy (or persistence) and amiability. Second, this is not an instrumental attitude, so that forbearance is the best way to achieve one's ends. The exercise of virtue must be its own end; that is, it does not necessarily lead to rewards, even though it will produce its own confirmatory evidence. Jane Austen tells a good story, but one could as easily imagine other, less romantic or satisfactory endings, according to the principles she discerns.

I point this out because Austen in fact portrays a very dark world, filled with all sorts of fates. The point of the story is not the outcome, but how a person of little power and necessarily limited insight conducts themselves when surrounded by forms of folly, and lack of insight, and advice that is not for the best, and even the deceptions practised by various seducers, who resemble the rest of the cast in appearance, but have their own hidden agendas.

This could be construed as a nightmarish world, full of doubt and snares, but that is not Austen's point, which is rather that the world is unavoidably mixed, and that we are inevitably vulnerable. The virtues she describes allow a person to live well in this mixed and vulnerable state, to make something good out of it in the company of others, and also, importantly, not to reject those others, for they alone contain the resources a person has. Austen's vision is simultaneously realistic and, one might say, amiable – or, on the side of this fallen world.

This I think is the lesson of forbearance: the cultivation of the virtues – in which forbearance has its place – is the art of learning to live faithfully in this mixed world. We need to take cognizance of that in order to participate in the character of God, to explore in this life the resources it contains, and to share them. The virtues are the key to our becoming human.

16

The vice of Lust: politics, religion and sexuality

There is a twofold problem in discussing Lust, and the deadly sins in general. The first is that the outcome is known in advance: I am against them all (and so, I presume, are you). Part of the (idle) interest of such a series is to see how a preacher reaches such a foregone conclusion without either showing himself to be utterly out of touch with contemporary society or, on the other hand, conceding too much and presenting what looks like an apology for sin. I am on a hiding to nothing. There is, moreover, a basic problem with the word 'sin': a good many people distrust it, for it has a robust certainty about it that fits ill with an age where the best lack all conviction, including conviction of sinfulness.

The second problem is that the notion of a sin, such as lust or envy or sloth, needs a context. We all live in a particular society, at a particular time; among other things, we live in a society where the notion of sin tends to be contested, or explained away, and so to understand what such notions might mean in practice we need to situate them, to give them a history where they live and take on recognizable forms. So instead of talking about the wickedness of our hearts, and how the gift of sexuality ought to be used responsibly (which are matters I believe in), I have decided to try to define the context and to sketch what I shall call a 'politics of lust' – and thus break all the rules of etiquette at once, which deem that one should not discuss politics, nor religion, nor sexuality; I am going to link all three.

A political experiment

About two hundred years ago, in 1792, the French king, Louis XVI, was put on trial and, in January of the following year, was guillotined. His execution brought to a formal end an extremely long political experiment, and in many respects inaugurated the modern age which we inhabit still. I am, of course, simplifying, but I am trying to tie down some quite complicated matters. The political experiment, which was rapidly named the 'Old Regime', was a hierarchical society in which each person found their place and their worth because the system as a whole was supposed to be consecrated by God: God's order and the social order were held to be one and the same. The real interest of this experiment lies in contrasting it with what came before it; ancient society was ordered upon a basis of masters and slaves, of persons and non-persons, of humans and chattels. The hierarchical society which was formally concluded in 1793, however, consisted only of persons, ordered by reciprocal duties and obligations, from the top to the bottom. It attempted to realize the insight that comes from the Jewish and Christian tradition that everybody is a person, for everyone is unique in the eyes of God.

Now this of course is an idealized view, but it is not completely so: many people at the time thought that in executing the king they were executing God's temporal representative, and the Revolution was accompanied by the sacking of churches, sacrilege and the murder of priests and religious as an everyday affair. These outbursts did not persist as part of the new state structure, but they gave expression to at least one thread in the Revolutionary mind – one indeed that derived from aristocratic thinking – which was the killing off of God in the conscience. Some of the preparatory work for the Revolution was done in the development of what is called 'free thought', in schemes that made man the measure of all social and moral order. The Revolution was then the realization of this thought in the political sphere, if only for a short while.

There was one person in the Revolutionary tumult who tried to take up this thinking and push it to its logical conclusions. This was the Marquis de Sade, who is infamous as a pornographic writer (and well worth avoiding, as such), but who also offers serious justifications for his writings; he is a philosopher of sorts. De Sade thought it was worth taking seriously the social order that results from killing the king, as the representative of God, and of making man and his desires the ceiling or limit to political and social organization. He did so in a thoroughly obsessive way, but then, so his letters tell us, he saw eighteen hundred people executed in front of his prison window in the space of five days, so excuses can be made for him.

He says two things. First, a society born out of the destruction of a God-ordered hierarchy must be based upon and permeated by crime – that crime is its truth. This I feel is a rather abstract point of view, but we will come back to it. Second, what comes to replace the former hierarchy is a society of masters and slaves, a return to the unmediated power of ancient society, where some are persons and others are not, but simply objects at the disposal of these persons. And he joins together these views in a savage parody of natural man – or integral man, as he calls him – which was the dominant ideological figure of the period.

Clearly, he says, society is now defined by man and his desires (and he by no means excludes women and their desires from this picture). All our desires and pleasures should be fulfilled, and since perversity heightens pleasure, and can only be natural, for it arises within us, it too should be given full rein. Moreover, society should be ordered politically in order that these pleasures should be pursued to the utmost. And this can be carried out because it is a natural truth that the strong dominate the weak, and the truth of such a society is criminality. This of course is offered by him in a spirit of bitter parody. He wrote a remarkable pamphlet, included in the middle of one of his books as part of the narrative, a pamphlet entitled 'Frenchmen! One More Effort if You Want to be Republicans!' in which he outlined these views, and pointed out that in such a society as he proposed, murder, cruelty, rape, abuse, sacrilege and so forth – all of which were being commonly practised at the time he was writing – should be regarded as social virtues, as the principles of social order. In short, he proposed a politics of lust, based upon the figure of natural man and the exclusion of God from the conscience.

A regime of desire

Now, de Sade was a lunatic or, perhaps it would be better to say, he raised parody to a lunatic level. Nevertheless, he tells us something about our own society – not the whole truth, clearly, but some sort of insight. Our society too is a modern one, where God has been, by and large, removed from the conscience – hence the embarrassment about the notion of sin – and has been replaced by 'natural man'. If we have a common model of the truth of humankind underlying politics, the media and everyday ideas, it is a vision of natural man and the goodness of his desires. I do not think that various competing visions of modern society differ in this respect. And sexual relations, which have every appearance of having become our highest good, are defined by the notion of the maximization of pleasure, which is a Sadean theme.

We are more confused than de Sade about the relationships between power and pleasure; his central hypothesis of criminality being the truth of that relationship does not have to be accepted, but at least he has the merit of resolving the contradiction between the maximizing of pleasure on the one hand and exploitation and abuse on the other. Because of our failure to recognize this contradiction, we live in a world where criminal expressions of sexual pleasure – in rape, for example, and child abuse – are continually agonized over, apparently with little understanding and to little effect.

Those movements set up in opposition to the dominant modes of sexuality in society tend not to escape from the same framework, for they too make sexual desire a central theme to their politics, and are therefore concerned with questions of power: who is free to pursue their pleasure? Anyone who flees from the lusts given rein in conventional society, despising its hypocrisy and power games, is liable to find the same problems transformed in those movements of liberation to which he or she has turned for help. And this is the story of any Sadean heroine: of virtue abused at every turn.

Discretion and human respect

I appear to have talked myself into a corner, by suggesting that current trends in sexual ethics, whether conservative or radical, share the same flawed – indeed, Sadean – basis. But there are other bases available, or that may be discovered, and I want briefly – and inadequately – to indicate two notions I have been trying to explore to counterpose to the themes I have identified.

These notions I term 'discretion' and 'human respect'. To take the first, it seems that for humans to be fully human they have to be allowed a degree of privacy. This is a public matter to the extent that how much private space is allowed is effectively a collective decision. At the moment, the topic of sexual desire is thoroughly public, for both commercial and political reasons, and it needs to be 'decommercialized' and 'depoliticized'. Discretion needs to be counterposed to what I have called a politics of lust. We cannot endlessly go on discussing, in the media and elsewhere, questions of desire and power, of who is allowed to do what, when, with whom. The discussion needs to be brought to a close, by and large, and without resolving all those burning questions we so much enjoy.

On the other hand, public restraint needs to be matched by private restraint; it is no use promoting discretion if it is simply to be a cloak for the exploitation of the weak. So we need some sort of concept of human respect, something that lies beyond the maximizing of pleasure as the only human good, and that has something to do with the human conscience, and the reawakening of God in the conscience. That is, conscience defined as something over and above our desires, to be recognized by its power of contradicting, not confirming what we want. I can see no other way of holding on to the insight of the irreducible importance of every person. The Christian contribution is to be made in this area: in insisting upon the universality of personality rather than its being a property of only a few.

The resources for this are present, for every group in society has notions of conscience and personality – however ill articulated – as well as notions of power and desire; hence, indeed, their moral fervour. What we need is the elaboration, on the basis of these resources, of a general politics of restraint rather than a politics of lust, a politics of discretion and human respect. This may be, in the contemporary frame, a specific contribution which the Christian calling can make to the common good.

17

Ways of living together: a perspective on Christian marriage

One of the crucial resources offered by the Christian faith is what we might call 'ways of character formation'. These are small-scale social processes, capable of being repeated and sustained, which create and shape people to live Christian lives. This is the purpose of the Eucharist and the Daily Offices. It is also the purpose of Christian marriage, which is, indeed, the commonest form of discipline within which ordinary lives may be brought to contribute to a wider good, through the development of Christian character and the exploration of Christian virtues.

A perspective which relies upon development and change involves sacrifice of the self, for the persons involved are altered through their participation. And such a process is not readily grasped or understood in a modern context, for we tend to think that people, at whatever stage of life they have reached, are in some sense complete. A notion of perfectibility, especially through work undertaken with others, goes against our current ideas of the essential person, who may need therapy to discover their true self, but does not need to give up their self in order to attain their heart's desire.

This invisibility of the idea of formation, and of practices of formation, affects discussion of the family, and has meant, more or less, the exclusion from public debate of consideration of the place of marriage in the formation and maintenance of the family.

My interest in the topic was reawakened by my being involved, in the summer of 2004, in some discussions concerning the appropriate boundaries to be set to the state's involvement with the family. The topic came indirectly from the National Family and Parenting Initiative, set up when the Labour government came to power in 1997. You may imagine that in such discussions, there are enthusiasts who believe that state provision should supplement almost every aspect of family life, especially with respect to the upbringing of the young. And equally, there are doubters who imagine that families should be left to their own devices, except in the most exceptional circumstances. All the positions, however, ignore the place of marriage, which might have been thought relevant to discussions of the family and parenting. I presume they do so because it might be thought prejudicial to introduce it – and this is because the decision whether to marry or not is seen as a matter of individual preference, and not a matter of public policy.

Nevertheless, there is a religious dimension to the debate, in this sense. In either case, the opponents accuse the advocates of the other position of lacking realism or – to put it in theological language – of being blind to the question of sin. One side of the argument goes: 'The state is by its nature calculating and not generous, and therefore not capable of acting adequately in the place of parental love', while the other side responds: 'Anyone who imagines that the family unsupervised is a paradise is living in cloud-cuckoo-land.' The interest of the question of sin is that it raises the business of redemption: how do you move from the present, unsatisfactory state to a more satisfactory one?

Now, I don't want to follow this argument through, except to say that its solutions rest on two assumptions, neither of which I feel entirely comfortable with. The first is the assumption that a major way to alter the state of society is to affect family relations, or, in other words, family relations are a key to social order. (In parody, this is the 'Do you blame the teachers or do you blame the parents?' conundrum.) The second is the assumption that the state is the right and the only agent to make these alterations, and that it is benign and trustworthy. The whole question of the place of civil society is conjured away. Both these assumptions are, I think, more myth than fact, and therefore not a good base or description from which to move towards social policy. And this is in part because they lack any notion of a mechanism for dealing with sin.

And the issue of a mechanism for dealing with sin brings us to the question of marriage or, at least, to Saint Paul's views on marriage. For he puts dealing with sin at the heart of the institution of marriage. One can do worse than start from 1 Corinthians 7.8–9, where he writes as follows: 'To the unmarried and the widows I say that it is well for them to remain single as I do. But if they cannot exercise self-control, they should marry. For it is better to marry than to be aflame with passion.' We shall see why in a moment.

This point of view commands little general support at present. And yet it contains a significant strand in the complex idea of Christian marriage. Given contemporary assumptions, outlined above, and the impasse that quickly develops in any discussion of the family along the lines they lay down, Paul's insight concerning sin and marriage may make a genuine contribution, since marriage is certainly linked – in the tradition, at least – to the formation of families.

The Prayer Book marriage service

Even so, we have to pick our liturgy of marriage. I shall turn to the 1662 Prayer Book, for which Saint Paul's thinking is central. If you look at the Preface to the 'Form of Solemnization of Matrimony', you will see that families – or rather, children – are the first justification given for the institution of marriage. The Preface in fact offers three 'causes for which Matrimony was ordained', and they are worth citing in full, for our purposes.

> First, [Matrimony] was ordained for the procreation of children, to be brought up in the fear and nurture of the Lord, and to the praise of his holy Name.
>
> Secondly [this is pure Saint Paul], It was ordained for a remedy against sin, and to avoid fornication; that such persons as have not the gift of continency might marry, and keep themselves undefiled members of Christ's body.
>
> Thirdly, It was ordained for the mutual society, help and comfort, that the one ought to have of the other, both in prosperity and adversity.

Some comments are in order on each cause.

First, as earlier forms of marriage had seen, the institution is necessary for creating the next generation, rather than simply the scattering of offspring, if I may put it so. This is the first reason why marriage is of public interest. It concerns the transmission of property and the continuation of social order; in this way, it contains elements of social flourishing, or public good, which may foretell salvation.

Second, earlier forms had also contained the next element – marriage as a remedy against sin. The Prayer Book, however, is a Reformation document, and it is worth noticing the interpretation it puts on the idea. Previously, for a period, women had been perceived as a potential source of mortal sin to men, and marriage as a way of preventing men's damnation. Women were instruments in this view, and not a lot more – instruments either of a man's condemnation (through the temptation to fornication) or his salvation (through marriage). This is not the view of the Prayer Book, however, and in this it is true to Saint Paul, who is extremely even-handed in his view of the participation of both sexes in God's purposes, and also of their equal propensity to sin.

This egalitarianism is borne out by the third cause cited, which is essentially that of companionship between the sexes. It is worth remarking that this is, effectively, a new emphasis.

Again, this is not a line I wish to pursue very far. It is however worth remarking that almost everybody nowadays earnestly subscribes to the view that women have souls just as do men, and also that they are not instruments with respect to men, that women and men are equal in the eyes of God, and that the proper relationship between men and women is one of companionship and partnership – 'mutual society, help and comfort', as the Prayer Book has it. I believe that, wholeheartedly. But I would also point out that, once such views are adopted, such issues as separation and the breakdown of the family – divorce, in a word – also come to the fore, because one party (or sex) cannot be sacrificed to the interests of the other. And the modern world, with all its woes and confusions, comes into being, as many writers contemporary to the Reformation saw. Nevertheless, Saint Paul's analysis has something to contribute here too, concerning how to live in such a world.

So it is the second cause I wish to focus on – the notion of marriage as a remedy for sin, which clearly echoes the verse given above. What is Paul saying? Why is the paragraph there, citing him, in the marriage service?

We are told in the paragraph preceding it in the Preface that this 'holy estate . . . is commended by Saint Paul to be honourable among all men: and therefore is not by any to be enterprised, nor taken in hand, unadvisedly, lightly, or wantonly, to satisfy men's carnal lusts and appetites, like brute beasts that have no understanding; but reverently, discreetly, advisedly, soberly, and in the fear of God'.

I may say, this language has been greatly objected to, and even ridiculed. People did not like being compared, even potentially, to 'brute beasts which have no understanding' (it is also disrespectful to beasts, no doubt, to suggest they lack understanding). Nor did they like its being suggested that intercourse might be linked to sin. And the more modern Anglican liturgies have therefore attenuated this emphasis, so that only the slightest hint remains. No more wantonness, carnal lusts, or brute beasts, only the quiet reminder that 'none should enter into [marriage] lightly or selfishly but reverently and responsibly in the sight of almighty God' (*Common Worship*: The Marriage Service). Even the 'a' of 'almighty God' is in lower case.

Marriage as an ascetic practice

Nevertheless, beyond the problem of the language adopted, Paul is trying to say something quite interesting, and what it is becomes clearer from the context of the seventh chapter of 1 Corinthians. In essence, he is concerned with how people best live lives that follow God, how they become disciples. This, in his view, involves a practice that shapes the person and their possibilities and their interactions with others, so that, in the process, they become evidence for God and live godly lives. He is concerned, in a technical term, with 'asceticism', from the Greek verb meaning 'to work': the work of forming a person.

Paul is quite clear that desire can be overpowering, that it can obstruct the growth of the love of God in a person, and that it can be enormously destructive of human good. Desire therefore needs ordering, so that it is rightly directed, towards God, and so that it has effects for good in those around and not bad.

The institution of marriage, in Paul's account, is such an ascetic practice. It is an ordering of desire, and as such it has outcomes – the production of children, the avoidance of forms of destructive behaviour, such as fornication, and the positive benefits of mutual companionship, forming a society from which others may also gain. These outcomes, we might notice, are all social, in that they involve third parties, for positive good or the avoidance of ill. That is, marriage is a settlement between the couple of whom further parties are beneficiaries.

That is the primary reason why marriage is a social institution: it is an aspect of the building up of a good social order, for it contributes to a public good; indeed, it helps to form this order and develop this good. It is not a way of manipulating social relations, as the modern, legislative attitude would hold; rather, it contributes to the public good because at the centre of it lies a practice or discipline – the formation not only of the self for good, but also of a good for others, through a right ordering of desire.

In this perspective, marriage is not unlike other godly disciplines concerned with the formation of social persons, and as such bears parallels with Daily Prayer, and could be conceived of as a form of worship. Yet this is a perspective we have almost entirely lost sight of when we speak of marriage. We tend to think that it is a natural good to make love, and that this can be carried out without institutions. We then have to have recourse to other institutions to deal with the unintended consequences of this somewhat pagan ethic.

And it is worth emphasizing that even contemporary Christian accounts of marriage tend to build upon this view, along the lines that the expression of our natural selves must be virtuous and godly. We simply then add in a rider that marriage is the best place for such expression, but we lack compelling arguments as to why.

Yet marriage might better be viewed not as the context for erotic relations, but rather as the subordinating of such relationships to other ends. Through godly discipline, a man and a woman order their natural desires to promote various forms of public good, whether it be of children, of others, or of one another. At the heart of this institution lies a discipline of sacrifice, of removing the ego or self from the centre of action and motive, and being at the service of specific others. Which is, it should be well understood, a proper path to happiness, and even bliss.

It is worth adding at this point that celibacy, consciously entered into as a similar godly practice, aims at an entirely comparable discipline. Understanding marriage along the lines outlined brings with it a positive account of non-marriage.

Wider implications

The reasons I have bothered to explore the topic this far are these.

First, there are public dimensions to these questions that are quite far-reaching. It is possible to claim that a person schooled in self-effacement and discipline might well be a good candidate for public office and responsibility. Or, to put it the other way round, holding office, or relating to the public good at any level, involves a person being schooled in the control of desire, so that some sort of objective or decentred account of any situation demanding response may be worked on. We assume such discipline in any public figure, but we rarely ask how such selfless persons are to be achieved. An ordered private life – or rather, many such – may make a real contribution to an ordered public life.

Second, such an account raises the question of the importance of institutions other than the state or the individual. Reliable persons are made at a scale that is neither singular nor general, but somewhere in between, in small groups which are formed through alliance, and descent, and proximity. There is a point, one might say, to civil society in general, and to families in particular, where the disciplines that form persons are passed on.

And third, these disciplines and their transmission have a lot more to do with the Church than is generally recognized. At their heart lies the right ordering of desire, and that appears to have to do with worship. In essence, Paul says put God at the centre, and everything else will follow. This programme needs a good deal of working out, but that is the key, and one of the ways it is worked out is through the institution of marriage.

This notion of a discipline of desire, or of forming habits of desire, then gives an edge to the Christian view of marriage which it will otherwise lack. It enables the Church to make a specific contribution to a series of contemporary discussions, and to raise certain issues that are otherwise obscured in these discussions. And it might even help with formulating our terms in the various debates which torment the Church about facets of human sexuality.

So let us follow Saint Paul, no longer resembling brute beasts with no understanding, but seeking to act reverently, discreetly, advisedly, soberly, and in the fear of God.

18

Rumours of hope

———◆———

Let me begin from Anthony Hurst's opinionated and thoroughly read- ·
able essay on the history of Southwark Diocese,[1] for it allowed me to
draw together and articulate certain impressions and themes.

That essay brings out various characteristics of the diocese, in particular its diversity: the continual growth and change of the population
in the last century, and the extraordinary range of parishes that result,
and what might be found in them – far more varied than in most
dioceses. It also brought out the feature of being 'London' – part of the
capital, at the centre of things, busy (as the police say), and with an exceptional spectrum of talents and concerns with which to engage. At the
same time, the diocese is also south of the river, with all that implies,
in contradistinction to London north of the river.

The notion of the 'South Bank' is itself of interest, because it indicates how long questions of finding forms for the contemporary expression of Christianity have been at the heart of the diocese (at least since
Cyril Garbett's time, it seems).[2] As a counterpart to those questions, the
notion points simultaneously to an equal engagement with the business
of faith making sense of contemporary culture and issues. In short, there
has been an enduring radical culture both of Christian expression and
exploration associated with Southwark Diocese.

The term 'South Bank Theology' was coined, as Hurst reminds us,
in 1963. The names of Mervyn Stockwood, John Robinson, Hugh
Montefiore, Nick Stacey and so forth were alive in my childhood and
growing up (in a theological household), and they are perhaps of particular interest to recall. They are worth recalling because they remind
us in particular of this curious pattern: that trying to adapt Christianity
to the contemporary world will cause extraordinary disturbances and
widespread interest, and that the disturbance is most acutely felt among
certain sections of the faithful.

That is to say, missionary activity tends to be undercut by reaction
and division within the home team. This is a recurrent pattern, which
needs quite careful consideration in order to do justice to the motives
being expressed by all parties. It is within the Church that the need to
engage with the world is felt most keenly and also that the cost of doing

so is paid. And it is clear why at a broad level, for adaptation and relevance can readily be perceived as dilution and loss. The whole business of making sense of the faith in this world, and the equal risk of ruining what has been handed on to us, divides us easily into tendencies and parties and factions – each one with part of the truth, for which part we are willing to sacrifice others. But if we are honest, I think, it also divides each one of us: we each contain the challenge and the risk, and bear the marks of the cost, and as such we have a good deal in common.

These kinds of issues – which are very Southwark, very South Bank issues – were expressed in the course of the Southwark Diocesan Clergy Conference, but only in the form of hints: glimpses, or rumours. What I might have expected, given what I know about South Bank Theology, and what I know about London south of the river, and what I heard around the conference, was a firmer declaration of their presence. Let me introduce them: they are poverty, sex, race and politics.

These issues do not have to be the cause of quarrels. Quietness is part of an Anglican process of discernment – the commitment that we belong together, with all our heartfelt differences, in a project under God and through Jesus Christ, in order that we might, possibly, come to agree. We do not have to agree in order to belong; the importance of the project trumps and holds together our differences. That position comes out of the Anglican settlement; it is a very great achievement of the Christian Church to have a political form that holds together differences intensely held; and it is true to Saint Paul's view of the Church, and to that of the epistle to the Ephesians.

Anglicanism is, however, based upon two broad principles, I believe. One is based in an understanding of the mystery of God, which is always greater than our partial vision and grasp on the truth. So we can with integrity belong in a common project with other people of integrity who differ from us in serious ways.

The other is based in the Incarnation, which announces that – contrary to all Greek expectation – God's character and purposes can be fulfilled in matter and history. That is why – stepping over several stages in the argument – we have a local, parochial system. We do not just agree to be in some sort of Christian solidarity with other believers, but also we take on a certain responsibility of care and mission for all the people in a given area. We do not choose those among whom we are sent to minister and so our agenda is set, in large part, by the area in which we serve.

And I am willing to bet that that agenda will include issues of economics (including poverty), and of sex (since nobody escapes that), and of identity (including interfaith matters, race and immigration), and of politics (or its failure). I know this, partly because I have read Anthony Hurst's essay.

These were the issues posed, often quite crudely, by the likes of Messrs Stockwood, Stacey, Montefiore and Robinson, in their efforts to promote a Christianity that makes links with the contemporary world. They may have been extreme in their attempts (they were, after all, intellectuals), and they may have met with indifferent success, but they were not wrong to try. Indirect evidence for that assertion lies in the Windsor Report, for there the issues of sex, politics, identity and economics are all linked one with another, mutually implicated. The lesson is that, in practice, the Church cannot escape dealing with these issues. Even if you turn your back on the issues in the parish, and have recourse to the policy known as 'liturgy and lethargy', or to various cognate forms, they will return, through the letterbox and in the politics of the Church.

I want now to go back over the issues that lie behind the Windsor Report.[3] I wish to do so in order to offer a description which brings out the mutually implicated nature of the issues. It offers a case study of complexity, and allows me to pose the issue of the complex world we live in, and in which you minister, without pretending to have an insight into the life of each of your parishes – which I cannot have. It is also a case study which ought to make you proud, for it indicates that what Southwark takes up as its agenda today, the Church will take up about forty years later.

Having looked briefly at this case study, I then want to ask, if life is like this, then how do we respond? How do we act in such a complicated world? What are our resources for integrity rather than play-acting, for confidence rather than contestation, for renewal rather than burn-out? In short, how do we enjoy our calling, rather than suffer it, and how might we describe that calling?

A case study

This then is my case study, which we might take in the form of a guided meditation. Imagine yourself back in the summer of 2003; you have just been appointed as a member of the Lambeth Commission chaired by Robin Eames, which has been set up to consider the consequences for the Anglican Communion of the consecration of Gene Robinson as Bishop of New Hampshire. These are your briefing notes.

Liberal Anglicans in the Episcopal Church of the USA (ECUSA) take the issue of ordaining as bishop a self-acknowledged homosexual to be one of integrity: such a man, by being true to his nature, is being true to God's will for him; his honesty is evidence of his merit. Opponents claim that such a position takes no account of the place of sacrifice, perfectibility and mutual responsibility.

Yet one cannot remain with a reading of the problem at a level of sexual ethics. It might be more useful to see the issue of homosexuality as connected at a level of signs to liberalism, economic and otherwise. Individualistic self-expression in sexual matters is associated with the free market, and the power of capital to express itself no matter what the cost to others. Homosexual expression is associated with Western cities and Western countries, and with Western economies. This is despite the fact that homosexuals within these cultures see themselves as marginal figures, and also that homosexuality is widely practised in other cultures; in a global economy, they are seen as a face of (to put it in an extreme way) Yankee Imperialism.

In this perspective, ECUSA's recent behaviour bears parallels with US government policy. ECUSA's conservative wing has been using the worldwide Anglican Church for some years to fight battles they are losing on the home front. And the liberal wing has acted without any regard for wider consequences. In neither instance is there much evidence of any global Anglican ways of thinking – of the autonomy of provinces counterbalanced by mutual responsibility.

Responses to ECUSA's actions vary according to local circumstances. Along the Christian–Muslim interface, bishops emphasize the consequences of the failure to take that mutual responsibility into account (martyrdom and church burning). Elsewhere, it is possible to take a more relaxed attitude, and to play down the significance of US moves (e.g. South Africa).

It is worth adding that homosexuality has always been taken up as a symbol pointing to other issues. The accusation has been used as an insult and as a way of labelling others. Under these conditions, it is not possible to reach a settlement as to what kinds of behaviour are prescribed, and what kinds are acceptable.

Therefore, any attempt to promote a reasonable ethical response – of such a kind as learning to live responsible sexual lives, with elements of discretion and human respect, a mix of privacy and accountability, neither being a cause for scandal nor allowing such freedoms to be a cover for selfishness – such an attempt cannot answer, for it will look like an apology for Western aggression.

In this context, one major question is, where does the Church wish to signal its solidarity? It is arguable that the Christian option should lie publicly with the wretched of the earth and not simply the wealthy; yet the former are rather conservative in their interpretation both of the Bible and of sexual ethics. One should not confuse this option with the resolution of pastoral problems in Western cities, and the local unease these resolutions engender in neighbouring dioceses. Yet these quite local conflicts have gained a considerable momentum and are causing distortion. Why is there this apparent lack of judgement locally?

We might notice a contrast in behaviour between English bishops, who are appointed, and ECUSA bishops, who are elected. In Britain, bishops and other diocesan officials, whatever their views, for the most part seek to act as a focus of unity, and conflictual politics comes mostly from successful parish priests and independent organizers, employed for example in theology colleges. In the States, bishops are elected and thereby mandated to represent positions. In the US, the factional leaders are more highly placed. (African bishops, we might remark, have yet a third kind of representative function.)

Mandated leaders have an interest in creating crises, both to establish authority and to show their followers they are delivering the goods. Congregations both in the UK and the States appear by and large to be indifferent to the issues, perplexed, unhappy at the prospect of splitting, and yet willing to be led by their pastors. There is potentially quite a conflict of interest between factional leaders and their followers.

Under these circumstances, the critical leaders are unlikely to be swayed in the long term by appeals to Christian virtues, unity, common baptism and so forth. Rather, the responses have to contain elements of carrot and stick: there have to be high practical costs to splitting (and their followers have to understand them), and there have to be real rewards for staying in.

What form does your response take? What are your proposals?

Working in complex situations

The virtue of such an exercise is that it shows how these elements I have identified – poverty, race, politics and sex – are present and bound to one another, in the interplay between local situations and their wider contexts. It exemplifies the complexity of the issues. And it helps us to understand how these same elements are also present, equally entangled, in the local situations in which you work. Every situation implies wider frames of reference; that is in part why they are difficult to talk about.

This situation also poses a quite technical problem, which I will put as follows. If you are an Anglican priest set in a parish with these sorts of issues at work in it, how are you to respond and minister without being baffled, and so reduced either to single-issue politics, or simply to minding your own business, so that you become engaged solely with running your church?

Faced with the problem of complexity, a management consultant would point to the need, not for a single blueprint or solution, but for a process or technique by which one learns to see the situation more clearly or which, in theological terms, purifies desire. For the issue under the conditions we describe is not strong leadership, but finding a way so that the people charged with taking responsibility for making decisions leave their egos and confusions and fears out of it, and take the necessary time and develop the appropriate division of labour and so forth, so that the ways forward which are proposed develop the situation, creating new possibilities rather than reproducing the old problems.

In the Church we have specific methods to achieve such purification, and these are the forms of worship – the Daily Offices and the Eucharist. These are essentially 'ascetic' practices, the formation of persons for discipleship. In the case of the Daily Offices, this process works through the meeting together of particular persons, bearing their own agendas, histories, responsibilities and desires, and their being read – confronted, comforted and built up – by Scripture. In this fashion, representative persons are construed by the mind of God. The process works differently in the Eucharist – meeting with the Lord, crucified and risen, though Scripture plays its part – but what is at stake in either case is a collective, small-scale, repeated ascetic practice, leading to the formation of persons, who will then serve as evidence of God's work in the world.

There are other such practices in the Christian tradition – notably and most widespread, marriage, a discipline of desire pursued for a public good – but the Offices and the Eucharist are the ones that are central to the priestly formation. Although not exclusive to priests: the practices should indeed be widespread.

This practice of daily worship is central to the discipline of Anglicanism as described, of belonging together and being at the service of a parish (or other places). And it is also how many oppositions – in particular that between the integrity of the person and the demands of the role – are resolved.

In conclusion, I want to consider a model of being a priest that might correspond to this account of daily worship as ascetic practice, in order too to see whether it is possible to move beyond this pragmatic stage (of how to respond to complexity) and glimpse what we might call the recovery of prophecy, or the ability to speak meaningfully into this complexity. In this way I might fulfil my brief, which was to speak of rumours of hope.[4]

The three features of being a priest I would call attention to are these: attentiveness, thankfulness and description. They are three faces of a single task or vocation.

I mentioned that the process of Morning Prayer works on its participants as representatives, in that we bring in agendas, connections, responsibilities and nesting involvements. Part of the outcome of the process, as the mind of God works in us, is an increasing engagement in our representative roles, which are different in every person and every parish. Three points may be made.

First, this process of attentiveness demands an extraordinary amount of work. In common with all laypersons, we are involved in a context, we gain experience through that involvement, we learn by reflecting upon that experience. That is already work. Our unique contribution is reading that involvement, experience and so forth through confrontation with Scripture in prayer, and that is not easily achieved, and this confrontation demands we return to that cycle of experience, reflection and so on. It is in short an ongoing project.

Second, because learning about the complex world we are engaged with (or that portion thereof) is hard work, and the work is never completed, we are always being tempted to retreat into piety, or single-issue politics, or church organization, or whatever, and to seek for magical short cuts.

Third, at least a partial answer to these difficulties lies in the division of labour: in sharing the work, relying on the expertise of others, being open to the experience and wisdom of fellow-Christians, and even of other people of good will but of little practising faith.

In short, cultivating the art of attentiveness means taking the world into prayer, and taking out of prayer the need to understand better that world – in order, among other things, to pray for it.

The second aspect of priesthood considered along these lines concerns thankfulness. One way of understanding worship is as gratitude. For one face of attentiveness, or what we might call godly attentiveness, to the world is a suspension of judgement. This is a large topic; all I can say now is that how one learns to see the world well is linked to learning to trust in God's providence and dispositions for humankind. Discernment is connected with the detachment of desire and with thankfulness to God. Again, this is a discipline – collective and hard-won – and not a cheerful irresponsibility and an endorsement of evils. Christians are rightly noted for their engagement in projects of social justice, but condemnation of others is less of a Christian calling, in large part because the gospel is good news for all, and not just for some. We bear witness by our positive acts, not by our negative judgements, and that is not a straightforward matter; at the heart of resolving it lies thankfulness, as a key to holiness.

The third feature concerns description. A church, whether local or national, which brings together a discipline of scriptural holiness and attentiveness to the world in the form hinted at might in due course produce descriptions of aspects of the world which would both surprise that world and make sense to it. The briefing I offered above for the Windsor Report is a primitive attempt at such a description, as is, in a different way, the account of the Daily Offices offered elsewhere. Priests pay attention, give thanks, and offer descriptions – on the basis of which action follows, or which are embodied in responsive action.

Good description offered by critical Christian minds would indeed in the end be prophetic. If we produced such descriptions, the Church would be far more engaged with society, it might well draw more people to participate in it, and it would certainly draw far more sustained hostility than it does at present.

The Church would still only offer rumours of hope, glimpses of glory. It of course does that today, but it could do more. However, short cuts, or attempts to hasten the process without serving the necessary apprenticeships, resolve nothing.

In brief and in sum, in a world where certainties of a metaphysical order have retreated, and lesser, competing certainties simply define the problem, the issue for us is to return to practices that have served well in the past, and so can be tried again (although with no guarantee of success), and which are within our compass to achieve, for we have the resources to sustain and explore them, in penny numbers or greater.

These resources are exploring Scripture, reading the Bible in worship, paying attention to the world, and waiting for the Lord.

Notes

1 Tradition, moderation, kindness and chaplaincy

A talk given to the tutors' colloquium at Nottingham University, 7 October 1989.

2 An Anglican vocation: chaplaincy as an experiment in providence

Report to the AGM of the Anglican Staff Association, University of Nottingham, 28 November 1991.

1 Austin Farrer, *A Celebration of Faith* (London: Hodder & Stoughton, 1970), pp. 26–35.

3 Community and vocation

A paper written for the Diocese of Southwell Vocation Advisors Group, 28 December 1991.

1 Alasdair MacIntyre, *After Virtue* (London: Duckworth, 1981).
2 These are the principal works used in the preparation of this paper: Joseph Butler, *The Analogy of Religion Natural and Revealed* [1736] (London: Dent, 1908); Samuel Taylor Coleridge, *Confessions of an Inquiring Spirit* [1840] (Menston: Scolar Press, 1971); David E. Jenkins, *Living with Questions* (London: SCM Press, 1969); Alasdair MacIntyre, *After Virtue* (London: Duckworth, 1981); Ian Ramsey, *Religious Language* (London: SCM Press, 1957); Rowan Williams, *The Wound of Knowledge* (London: Darton, Longman & Todd, 1979).

4 Church and intellectuals, nation and state

Published in *Theology*, vol. 98, no. 792 (Nov.–Dec. 1996), pp. 452–6.

1 Cf. Bernard Crick, *In Defence of Politics* (Harmondsworth: Penguin, 1962).
2 An observation borrowed from Rowan Williams.
3 Cf. Alexis de Tocqueville's description of the last days of *The Ancien Régime* [1856] (London: Dent, 1988).

5 Two charisms: the Toronto blessing and the ordination of women

From a sermon preached in Jesus College Chapel, Cambridge, April 1995.

1 Particularly from papers given by Philip Richter and Stephen Hunt.
2 This idea in particular I gained from Philip Richter's paper.

6 Buildings and saints: the Feast of Saint Etheldreda

A sermon preached in Ely Cathedral on the Feast of St Etheldreda, 1996; revised for this volume.

1 This and the following paragraph draw heavily upon Janet Soskice's article 'Resurrection and the New Jerusalem' for whatever inspiration they contain; I am also grateful to this article for the reference to Stookey – see n. 2.
2 See Laurence Hill Stookey, 'The Gothic Cathedral as the Heavenly Jerusalem: Liturgical and Theological Sources', *Gesta*, 8 (1969), pp. 35–41.
3 Stookey, 'The Gothic Cathedral', p. 37.
4 See C. J. Stranks, *Saint Etheldreda: Queen and Abbess* (repr. Loddon, Norfolk: Roberts & Son, 1989).

7 An ethical account of ritual: an anthropological description of the Anglican Daily Offices

Published in this version in *Studies in Christian Ethics*, 15 (2002), pp. 1–10.

1 Catherine Bell, *Ritual Theory, Ritual Practice* (Oxford: Oxford University Press, 1992).
2 For recent discussions, see Gilbert Lewis, *Day of Shining Red: An Essay on Understanding Ritual* (Cambridge: Cambridge University Press, 1980); Bell, *Ritual Theory*; Caroline Humphrey and James Laidlaw, *The Archetypal Actions of Ritual: A Theory of Ritual Illustrated by the Jain Rite of Worship* (Oxford: Oxford University Press, 1994); Talal Asad, *Genealogies of Religion: Discipline and Reasons of Power in Christianity and Islam* (Baltimore, Md.: Johns Hopkins University Press, 1993).
3 Cf. Charles Taylor, 'Social Theory as Practice', in Charles Taylor, *Philosophy and the Human Sciences: Philosophical Papers 2* (Cambridge: Cambridge University Press, 1985), pp. 91–115.
4 Consider the familiar list of topics, which constitute more or less an ethnographic checklist: beyond the Eucharist and the Daily Offices, we find the occasional offices of baptism, marriage and burial, the visitation of the sick, thanksgiving after childbirth, commination, the ordination of bishops, priests and deacons, forms of prayer and thanksgivings for the fertility of crops and for the right ordering of society, including Church and state, a table of kindred and affinity, plus the Litany, creeds and a catechism.
5 In an attempt to keep a clear distinction between the anthropological and the theological, I ignore the range of writing on the Offices from within the Church, to which, nevertheless, I owe a good deal, especially George Guiver, *Company of Voices: Daily Prayer and the People of God* (London: SPCK, 1988).

8 An approach to the Millennium or, the first millennium and the second

Published in *Theology*, vol. 102, no. 807 (May–June 1999), pp. 161–9, and revised slightly for this volume.

1 The points in this paragraph are taken from Edmund Leach, *Rethinking Anthropology* (London: Athlone Press, 1961), p. 125.

2 See Norman Cohn, *The Pursuit of the Millennium* (London: Secker & Warburg, 1957), ch. 1.

3 Michael Sadgrove, 'Religion, Society and the New Millennium', unpublished address, 19 February 1996.

4 See, for example, *The Independent* 'Review', 20 August 1998.

5 Cf. Jorge Luis Borges' remarkable story, 'The Lottery in Babylon' – in *Labyrinths* (ET Harmondsworth: – which explores some of the issues).

6 Quoted in Georges Duby, *The Three Orders: Feudal Society Imagined* [1978] (ET Chicago: Chicago University Press, 1980), p. 5.

7 To quote Duby, *The Three Orders*, p. 5.

8 Explored by Georges Dumézil in *Mythe et epopée*, vol. 1 (Paris: Gallimard, 1968).

9 Duby, *The Three Orders*, p. 5.

10 See Anselm, *Why God Became Man*, ed. Joseph M. Colleran (Albany, N.Y.: Magi Books, 1969).

11 One could also imagine, inversely, dating from a moment of disorder one never wished to repeat – After the Flood, After the War – but such a negative system would not endure in the same way.

9 Giving

Sermon preached in St Paul's Cathedral, 7 February 1999.

10 Living in the Promised Land

Talk delivered in Leicester Cathedral, 26 January 2005, based on sermons delivered in 1999 and 2000.

11 Sacred time

A talk given at the Fitzwilliam Museum, 9 February 2000, as part of the *Tempus* Exhibition, relating to the Millennium.

1 The following three paragraphs repeat material from Chapter 10.

12 Ecclesiastes, chapters 1—3

Sermons preached in Jesus College Chapel, Cambridge, October 2003.

1 I have used several works, but in particular two commentaries – James L. Crenshaw, *Ecclesiastes: A Commentary* (London: SCM Press, 1988) and Ellen Davis, *Proverbs, Ecclesiastes and the Song of Songs* (Louisville, Ky.: Westminster John Knox Press, 2000) – and a monograph by Michael V. Fox, *Qoholet and His Contradictions* (Sheffield: Almond Press, 1989). See also Michael Fox's *A Time to Tear Down and a Time to Build Up: A Re-reading of Ecclesiastes* (Grand Rapids, Mich.: Eerdmans, 1999).

13 Religion in English everyday life

Talk to Leeds University Theology Department, 16 May 2001.

1 Timothy Jenkins, *Religion in English Everyday Life: An Ethnographic Approach* (Oxford and New York: Berghahn), 1999.

2 The use of this published material (1) invokes the reflexivity of the processes by which local society is constituted under an intermittent metropolitan gaze, and (2) sketches an 'etymological' method by which the play of wide cultural forces in a situation can be accounted for and controlled in a scholarly way.

3 Timothy Jenkins, 'Fieldwork and the Perception of Everyday Life', *Man*, 29 (1994), pp. 433–55.

4 Cf. Conrad: 'a man's real life is that accorded to him in the thoughts of other men by reason of respect or natural love'.

5 I discuss these issues in an essay titled 'Congregational Cultures and the Boundaries of Identity', in Mathew Guest, Karin Tusting and Linda Woodhead (eds), *Congregational Studies in the UK* (Aldershot: Ashgate, 2004), pp. 112–23.

14 Anglicanism: the only answer to modernity

Published in Duncan Dormor, Jack McDonald and Jeremy Caddick (eds), *Anglicanism: The Answer to Modernity* (London: Continuum, 2003), pp. 186–205.

1 See Georges Duby, *The Three Orders* (ET Chicago, Ill.: University of Chicago Press, 1980).

2 John Neville Figgis, *The Divine Right of Kings* [1914] (Bristol: Thoemmes Press, 1994).

3 David Hume, *Essays* [1777] (Indianapolis, Ind.: Liberty Fund, 1985).

4 Michel de Montaigne, 'On Cannibals' [1580] (Harmondsworth: Penguin, 1958), pp. 105–19.

5 Stephen Toulmin, *Cosmopolis: The Hidden Agenda of Modernity* (Chicago, Ill.: University of Chicago Press, 1990).

6 Cf. the earlier account of the Anglican Daily Offices, Chapter 7.

15 Unfashionable virtues: forbearance

A sermon preached in Jesus College Chapel, Cambridge, 18 January 2004.

16 The vice of Lust: politics, religion and sexuality

A sermon preached at St Mary's, High Pavement, Nottingham, 22 March 1992.

17 Ways of living together: a perspective on Christian marriage

Published in *Crucible*, July–September 2005, pp. 14–19.

18 Rumours of hope

An address to the clergy of Southwark Diocese at the Southwark Diocesan Clergy Conference, 21 October 2004.

1 Anthony Hurst, *Diocese of Southwark 1905–2005: A Centennial Celebration* (London: Southwark Diocese, 2004).

2 Cyril Garbett was Bishop of Southwark from 1919 to 1932.

3 The Lambeth Commission on Communion, *The Windsor Report 2004* (London: Anglican Communion Office, 2004).
4 This account draws heavily upon discussions with friends, in particular with my Cambridge colleague Ben Quash.

The Society for Promoting Christian Knowledge (SPCK) was founded in 1698. Its mission statement is:

To promote Christian knowledge by

- **Communicating the Christian faith in its rich diversity;**
- **Helping people to understand the Christian faith and to develop their personal faith; and**
- **Equipping Christians for mission and ministry.**

SPCK Worldwide serves the Church through Christian literature and communication projects in over 100 countries, and provides books for those training for ministry in many parts of the developing world. This worldwide service depends upon the generosity of others and all gifts are spent wholly on ministry programmes, without deductions.

SPCK Bookshops support the life of the Christian community by making available a full range of Christian literature and other resources, providing support for those training for ministry, and assisting bookstalls and book agents throughout the UK.

SPCK Publishing produces Christian books and resources, covering a wide range of inspirational, pastoral, practical and academic subjects. Authors are drawn from many different Christian traditions, and publications aim to meet the needs of a wide variety of readers in the UK and throughout the world.

The Society does not necessarily endorse the individual views contained in its publications, but hopes they stimulate readers to think about and further develop their Christian faith.

For further information about the Society, visit our website at *www.spck.org.uk* or write to:
SPCK, 36 Causton Street,
London SW1P 4ST, United Kingdom.